Reading

Developmental Continuum

The Reading Developmental Continuum was researched, developed and written by Diana Rees, Education Officer, First Steps Project, Ministry of Education, WA, in collaboration with Dr Bruce Shortland-Jones, Curtin University of Technology.

First Steps was developed by the Education Department of Western Australia under the direction of Alison Dewsbury.

HEINEMANN
Portsmouth, NH

Heinemann
A Division of Reed Elsevier Inc.
361 Hanover Street
Portsmouth, NH 03801-3912

Offices and agents throughout the world

First published 1994 by
Addison Wesley Longman Australia
on behalf of the Education Department of Western Australia

Library of Congress Cataloging-in-Publication Data
CIP is on file with the Library of Congress.
ISBN 0-435-07253-6

Printed in the United States of America on acid-free paper
01 00 99 98 97   RRD   1 2 3 4 5 6 7 8 9

Contents

Part I

Foundations of First Steps

In this section the philosophical and theoretical framework of First Steps is set out. Specific points are made about the teaching of children for whom English is a second language and some suggestions are made about factors which foster effective learning in the classroom.

Foundations of First Steps includes:

- Linking Assessment to Teaching
    - The Developmental Continua
    - Teaching Strategies
    - Underlying Theoretical Assumptions
    - Important Considerations
    - Teaching Children for whom English is a Second Language

- Effective Learning
    - Problem Solving
    - Embeddedness
    - Working Memory
    - Interaction
    - Time

- 'The Three Rs'
    - Reflecting
    - Representing
    - Reporting

Linking Assessment to Teaching

In an increasingly complex world, re-evaluating methods of teaching and learning is important. At the same time, methods of evaluating development, especially in relation to testing, have become highly problematic. Effective teachers have always used systematic observation and recording as a means of assessment. The First Steps materials have been developed to give teachers an explicit way of mapping children's progress through observation. The Developmental Continua validate what teachers know about children.

The Developmental Continua

The continua have been developed to provide teachers with a way of looking at what children can actually do and how they can do it, in order to inform planning for further development. It is recognised that language learning is holistic and develops in relation to the context in which it is used. However, given the complexity of each mode of language, a continuum has been provided for reading, writing, spelling and oral language, in order to provide teachers with in-depth information in each one of these areas.

The Continua make explicit some of the indicators, or descriptors of behaviour, that will help teachers identify how children are constructing and communicating meaning through language. The indicators were extracted from research into the development of literacy in English-speaking children. It was found that indicators tend to cluster together, i.e. if children exhibit one behaviour they tend to exhibit several other related behaviours. Each cluster of indicators was arbitrarily called a 'phase'. This clustering of indicators into phases allows teachers to map overall progress while demonstrating that children's

language does not develop in a linear sequence. The concept of a phase was shown to be valid by the Australian Council for Educational Research in their initial research into the validity of the *Writing: Developmental Continuum*.

Individual children may exhibit a range of indicators from various phases at any one time. 'Key' indicators are used to place children within a specific phase, so that links can be made to appropriate learning experiences. Key indicators describe behaviours that are typical of a phase. Developmental records show that children seldom progress in a neat and well-sequenced manner; instead they may remain in one phase for some length of time and move rapidly through other phases. Each child is a unique individual with different life experiences so that no two developmental pathways are the same.

The indicators are not designed to provide evaluative criteria through which every child is expected to progress in sequential order. They reflect a developmental view of teaching and learning and are clearly related to the contexts in which development is taking place. That is, language development is not seen as a 'naturalistic' or universal phenomena through which all children progress in the same way. Children's achievements, however, provide evidence of an overall pattern of development which accommodates a wide range of individual difference.

Teaching Strategies

The other major purpose of these documents is to link phases of development to teaching strategies, in order to help teachers make decisions about appropriate practice in the light of children's development. It is important that within this framework teachers value individual difference and cultural diversity. **It is not intended that these** strategies are prescriptive; they offer a range of practices from which teachers might select, depending upon the purposes of any particular language program and the needs of the children in their class. The purpose of the Continua is to link assessment with teaching and learning in a way that will support children and provide practical assistance for teachers.

Underlying Theoretical Assumptions

The First Steps indicators and suggested activities have been based on the following theoretical assumptions:

- Language learning takes place through interactions in meaningful events, rather than through isolated language activities

- Language learning is seen as holistic; that is, each mode of language supports and enhances overall language development

- Language develops in relation to the context in which it is used; that is, it develops according to the situation, the topic under discussion, and the relationship between the participants

- Language develops through the active engagement of the learners

- Language develops through interaction and the joint construction of meaning in a range of contexts

- Language learning can be enhanced by learners monitoring their own progress

- The way in which children begin to make sense of the world is constructed through the language they use and reflects cultural understandings and values

It is important that the indicators and activities are interpreted from the perspective of these underlying assumptions about language learning.

Important Considerations

The First Steps materials have been designed to help teachers map children's progress and suggest strategies for further development. When making decisions about what to do next, there are a number of issues that need to be considered.

Teachers' actions, strategies and ways of interacting with children reflect particular values and assumptions about learning. Through these interactions, children construct a view of what 'counts' as literacy in a particular classroom setting. This is manifested in the way:

a) teachers make decisions about selecting materials and texts
b) activities are carried out using the materials and texts
c) teachers talk with children
d) children talk with each other
e) what gets talked about (topic)

The decisions made by teachers play a role in how children come to understand what counts as literacy. In some cases there may be major conflicting and competing value systems at work leading to a variety of outcomes.

For example, the text Cinderella implicitly constructs a particular view of the world which presents women in a stereotypical role, not necessarily reflecting the role of women in modern society.

Clearly the text can be used in a number of different ways. It might be used as a shared book experience in which the teacher engages the children in a reading of the text, developing talk around the concepts of print and the repeated patterns of the text. In focusing on these aspects, the teacher would be constructing a view of reading which places emphasis on print rather than the message and leaves the role of women, as presented in the text, unchallenged. However, if the teacher encouraged the children to talk about the text in a way that challenged this view, through talking about their own experience of women and presenting other literature, the teacher would begin the process of helping children to detect the values within text.

Moving from this activity to asking the children to draw a picture of their own siblings and write a description about them, the teacher's response will signal to children what is important. Focusing on spelling and grammar will indicate that correctness is valued above content, whereas focusing on the content by discussing the characteristics of their siblings and comparing these with the ugly sisters, enables the children to become 'critical' readers.

The teaching strategies that are used and the texts selected are very powerful transmitters of cultural knowledge and how children construct the task of learning to be literate. In relation to the texts selected, what seems to be critical is the way in which they are used, rather than merely trying to select the 'right' text, because all texts convey values of some sort.

Given that literacy learning is such a complex task, teachers will use a range of different strategies for different purposes according to the needs of the children. However, what seems to be important is that teachers are consciously aware of which strategies they are selecting, why, and how these actions will impact on the children's understanding of what counts as literacy.

Another aspect of decision making is related to recognition of the specific skills, attitudes and knowledge children bring to the classroom. In order to enable children to feel confident in their own abilities, it is important to recognise, value, consolidate and extend the diversity of children's competence through classroom practice.

When planning a language program which will put the suggested strategies from First Steps into practice, based on the knowledge gained through mapping the children's progress through the indicators, it may be useful to consider the following:

– What new ways of using and understanding language do you want children to develop?
– What sort of contexts will enable this development to occur?
– What sort of texts (oral, written, media, dramatic) will facilitate this learning?
– How will children need to be supported in processing these texts?

– What new skills, processing and knowledge might the children need explicit understanding of in order to complete the language task?
– What underlying values and assumptions encompass your literacy program?
– How will the interactions between you and the children facilitate your aims for literacy development?
– How can you help children to monitor their own progress?

Caroline Barratt-Pugh
Judith Rivalland

Teaching Children for whom English is a Second Language

(or children whose language of home differs from that of the teacher)

When teaching children for whom English is a second language it is important to recognise:

• the diversity and richness of experience and expertise that children bring to school

• cultural values and practices that may be different from those of the teacher

• that children need to have the freedom to use their own languages and to code-switch when necessary

• that the context and purpose of each activity needs to make sense to the learner

• that learning needs to be supported through talk and collaborative peer interaction

• that the child may need a range of 'scaffolds' to support learning and that the degree of support needed will vary over time, context and degree of content complexity

- that children will need time and support so that they do not feel pressured
- that supportive attitudes of peers may need to be actively fostered
- that it may be difficult to assess children's real achievements and that the active involvement of parents will make a great deal of difference, as will on-going monitoring.

Action Research in a wide range of classrooms over a four-year period indicates that effective teaching strategies for children for whom English is a second language and children whose language of home differs from that of the teacher are:

- Modelling
- Sharing
- Joint Construction of Meaning
- The provision of Scaffolds or Frameworks
- Involvement of children in self-monitoring of their achievements
- Open Questions

  Open Questions that are part of sharing or joint construction of meaning, e.g. questions such as 'Do you think we should do … or … to make it work?' or 'It was very clever to do that. How did you think of it?', are very helpful. When children are asked closed questions to which teachers already know the answers, such as 'What colour/shape/size is it?', children often feel threatened and tend to withdraw.

These factors are expanded in the 'Supporting Diversity' chapters in First Steps *Reading: Resource Book* and *Oral Language: Resource Book*.

Caroline Barratt-Pugh
Anna Sinclair

Effective Learning: PEWIT

Many factors enhance or inhibit learning. The following factors help children and adults learn effectively. They are reflected in the First Steps Developmental Continua and Resource Books and underpin all the teaching and learning activities.

- Problem-solving
- Embeddedness
- Working memory
- Interaction
- Time

Problem Solving

Effective learning occurs when children and adults are able to modify and extend their understandings in order to make sense of a situation which has challenged them. This is the essence of problem solving. Effective problem solvers are those who can:

- identify a specific concept or skill as one that is posing a problem
- decide to do something about it
- have a go at finding a solution, using a range of strategies
- keep going until they are satisfied that their new understandings or skills provide the solution they have been reaching for.

Children

Children are natural learners. Young children are constantly learning about their environment through interaction, exploration, trial and error and through 'having a go' at things. As a child's world of experience expands, so deeper understandings are constructed. Additional learning is always built upon existing foundations, and existing structures are constantly being adapted to accommodate fresh insights. Children use language to make sense of their world, imposing order on it and endeavouring to control it.

In coming to terms with the spoken and written language:

  (i) children need to see clearly the purposes for talking and listening, reading and writing so that they can adopt goals for themselves
  (ii) children are engaged in problem solving when they explore oral and written language in their environment, in play and in role-play
  (iii) children are problem solving when they attempt to represent the written language on paper
  (iv) children are problem solving when they attempt to represent oral language in print

Teachers

Teachers are faced with a multitude of challenges every day. How can a difficult concept be introduced? How can the classroom be constantly stimulating for children without risking teacher burn-out? How can a different management strategy be implemented without risk of losing control? How can new insights into gender equity be incorporated into the curriculum?

In implementing change, it is helpful if each challenge can be represented as a problem which can be solved using the technique of 'having a go'; trying out a strategy; reflecting on the result; and then having another go, having slightly modified the strategy, Teachers sometimes expect too much of themselves. They should not expect things to work perfectly first time round. The essence of problem-solving is that strategies and understandings are gradually refined over time. There is seldom one right or easy answer, but a whole range of solutions on a variety of levels that fit the children's needs, teachers' own personal styles and the demands of the tasks.

Embeddedness (Contextualisation)

Most people have had the experience of listening to a speaker and being totally unable to make sense of what is being said. In such circumstances one is apt to say 'I switched off. It didn't make a word of sense.' People need to be able to make connections between their own current understandings and new learning that is being undertaken. A person who knows nothing of mechanics may be quite unable to follow a lecture on car maintenance, but may be able to work things out if the car is there with the bonnet up and the parts clearly visible.

If the context and the problem are embedded in reality and make sense to the learner, then the learner can engage in productive problem solving. If the problem is not embedded in, and seen to be arising from, past experience, then rote learning may occur, but real learning, which is capable of generalisation, will probably not take place.

Children

Children learn effectively in contexts that make sense to them. The challenges which children face and the problems which they attack in their early environment are embedded in familiar, real life contexts. This can be seen quite clearly in early oral language development, when language acquisition is closely tied to the immediate environment and to current needs.

In coming to terms with written language:

(i) children need to be given opportunities to interact with print (read and write) in contexts which make sense to them and which have their counterpart in the real world, in role play and in real situations, e.g. making shopping lists, identifying stop signs

(ii) children need to see adults explicitly modelling reading and writing for a variety of purposes in real situations, e.g. reading and writing notes

(iii) children need to interact not only with books, but with the wide range of print found in daily life, e.g. in newspapers and environmental print.

Teachers

Teachers also need to start from where they are, working within their own familiar context. The First Steps resources offer a number of alternative ways of looking at teaching and a great many strategies and activities which people have found to be useful. Once teachers have decided what problem they want to solve or what challenge they wish to take on, they need to start from a context which makes sense to them and gradually incorporate alternative strategies within their own repertoires. The new learning needs to be embedded within the context of the old and teaching strategies need to be slowly adapted to meet new challenges and different understandings.

Working Memory (Mental Space)

Working memory, which is sometimes called M-space, is very different from long or short term memory. It is, in effect, a measure of the number of discrete elements which the mind can cope with at any one time. A good analogy is that of the juggler, who can juggle competently with four or five balls, but when given one too many, will drop the lot.

Once ideas and skills become familiar as a result of practice over a period of time, two things happen. One is that the learner does not have to think consciously about how to do them any more, so much less space is taken up in the working memory, e.g. spelling a very familiar word. The other is that several different skills gradually become one skill. For example when learning to print children have to manipulate the pencil, remember the formation of letters and consider the order in which the marks have to appear on the page. With practice these individual skills will integrate to become one skill.

Any emotional issue or concern will 'fill up' the mental space more quickly than anything else. Fear, anger or worry may totally inhibit a person's capacity to learn. Most people have had the experience of being unable to concentrate because their mind is fully taken up by an all-consuming emotion. The only thing to do is to give oneself time to 'get it together' again. In the meantime performance on any task will be poor and will continue to deteriorate until the cloud of emotion has lifted. If people say 'I just couldn't think straight', they are usually speaking the truth.

Children

Children focus their entire attention on one element which they perceive to be a challenge. Young children can only cope with one or two different factors at once. As they get older they can juggle with an increasing number of elements, although there is a limit to the amount that anyone can handle.

In coming to terms with the written language:

(i) children may only be able to focus on one or two different factors at any one time. For example, during a shared reading lesson one child may focus on the meaning and spelling of an unusual word in a story, whereas another may be emotionally involved with the characters. Neither may have 'heard' the teacher explaining the use of speech marks.

(ii) as they focus on one skill children may temporarily lose competence in another very familiar skill. For example when a child is absorbed in getting ideas onto paper the quality of handwriting may deteriorate.

(iii) children need to practise and apply a particular aspect of language in a number of contexts until it becomes automatic. Opportunities to practise in stimulating circumstances constitute an important component of all language programs, so that 'mental space' is made available for more complex learning.

(iv) children may appear to make significant regressions if their 'mental space' is fully taken up with an emotional issue relating to home or school.

Teachers

Teachers sometimes make impossible demands on themselves. They are also only able to cope with a certain number of new things at any one time. Instead of attempting everything at once, they need to try one small component of a task first and then build on that. For instance, it is impossible to attempt to observe all the children in a class at once. The secret is to focus on only three or four children a week, looking only at the key indicators. Children thought to be at risk can gradually be placed on the continuum, looking at all indicators.

It is important not to try to do too much at once. If circumstances become overwhelming for any reason, such as trouble at home, too many extraneous duties or ill health, teachers should wait for things to calm down before trying anything new.

Interaction

Interaction is of fundamental importance to human beings. People need to discuss ideas, build on each other's expertise, use each other as sounding boards and work creatively as communities of learners. It is through talk that ideas are generated, refined and extended.

Children

Children need unlimited opportunities to interact with adults and with other children in their daily lives. They need to interact with others to plan, explore, problem-solve, question, discuss and direct their activities. In doing so they try out and modify their ideas. As they use language in social situations they refine their language use and learn more about how language works.

In coming to terms with the written language:

(i) children need freedom to interact with adults in discussions about writing and reading. These discussions should not always be dominated by adults. Children need opportunities to direct conversation. The adult role may be to provide feedback and reinforcement.

(ii) children need freedom to interact with their peers to discuss problems and to formulate and clarify their ideas as they write

(iii) children need to feel safe to ask for help when they need it.

(iv) children need freedom to experiment with written language in socially supportive situations.

Teachers

Teachers also need time and opportunities to interact with their colleagues. Often the most profitable interactions take place informally between staff members who trust and respect each other. Time can also be put aside at a regular meeting for a school staff to discuss and share professional issues and insights regarding the implementation of First Steps or interesting new initiatives being undertaken by different teachers. One school developed a sharing strategy whereby every staff member concentrated on one specific strategy for a week or two, after which all reported back. This school took advantage of the wealth of expertise which is to be found in any staff room.

It is also extremely helpful to interact with parents informally as well as in more formal conferences to share insights about the children. Interacting with children is also of crucial importance, encouraging a two-way process which will enrich both teacher and child as each listens and responds to the other. Conferences between teacher, parent and child as co-members of the community of learners can also be very profitable.

Time

Children

In their everyday lives children have time to construct understandings gradually through inquiry, exploration and problem solving. They also have time to consolidate and integrate these understandings through practice. The amount of time needed to practise new skills and learnings

will vary from child to child. Some may need to apply these understandings in only a few situations before they come to terms with them. Others will need to apply the understandings more frequently and in a wider variety of situations before they can begin to generalise and transfer them.

In coming to terms with the written language:

(i) children need opportunities to have regular and on-going involvement in strategies such as shared book experiences, language experience and playing with language, in order to foster their understandings about how the written language works

(ii) children need opportunities to have regular involvement in activities which give them independent practice in their own time, at their own pace, as often as is needed in both reading and writing

Teachers

Teachers need to be as kind to themselves as they are to their children. They need to give themselves time for reflection; time for experimentation and having a go; time to refine and develop strategies already in place; time for sharing with colleagues and parents and time to enjoy their job. Every adult is growing and developing throughout life. Real growth takes time in every sphere of life and development can be enhanced but not hurried. Teachers need to be confident that they are comfortable with the strategies they are implementing and time will be on their side.

Effective Learning: 'The Three Rs'

Adults and children are all learners moving along a continuum. Teachers and children come together as a community of learners. All can benefit from the three Rs:

- Reflecting
- Representing
- Reporting

Reflecting

Children

Children need time to reflect on an experience and on what they have learned from it. Too often they hustle from one learning activity to another, with no time, no space and no structure to help them stand back and think about what they have learned. If they are encouraged to pause and reflect on the insights they have gained and on things that have suddenly started to make sense to them, they will consciously take control of their learning in a new way. They will develop an awareness of specific understandings and the place of those understandings in the overall scheme of things. They will come to value and respect themselves as learners and will become aware of their own learning processes.

Teachers

Teachers need to take time to reflect on their teaching practice. They need to congratulate themselves on their many successes, to consider their goals and take stock of their current situation. Studies have shown, for instance, that almost all primary school teachers firmly believe in developmental learning, but this is not always reflected in their approach to teaching. Teachers may reflect on their teaching practice by asking themselves questions such as: Are my beliefs and theoretical understandings reflected in my current classroom practice? Are the needs of all children being met? Are children engaged in active learning? Are they interacting effectively with others?

It is always worth taking time to reflect on the reality of daily classroom experience, to analyse strengths and to pin-point the areas that may need extra attention. Management strategies, interaction with parents, collaborative work with other staff members and teacher's own professional development are all areas which can provide food for thought from time to time.

Representing

Children

Children may need to represent their learning in a very concrete form. This may be by drawing a picture, constructing a diagram or by writing down their thoughts. In some learning areas such as maths or science it may involve constructing a model.

Teachers

Teachers may need to clarify their reflections by listing one or two items that seem to be significant. Even if no action is taken immediately, an insight will have been captured and recorded for future use. If an idea is written down it is likely to become a reality.

Reporting

Children

Children need to clarify their understandings by talking about them. Children refine, consolidate and extend their learning by reporting on what they know to a peer, a small group or their teacher. This type of reporting occurs best in a natural context when a child is not under any stress and does not feel 'on show.'

Teachers

Teachers may wish to contribute to the process of school planning by reporting on what they consider to be essential goals, strategies and issues for their schools and their students. Every staff member has a crucial contribution to make which will enrich and extend the operations of the school community. Too often the richness and depth of a teacher's experience is confined to one classroom instead of being available for all members of the educational community. All teachers need the support of every other teacher if children are to gain the full benefit of growing up in a community of learners.

Part II

About Reading

This section provides some general information about reading in the First Steps Program with emphasis on collecting data to help plan appropriate teaching strategies.

- Effective Communication
- What Do We Know About Reading?
- How to Use the Reading Developmental Continuum
  - Predict
  - Collect Data
  - Involve parents and children
  - Link Assessment with Teaching
  - Monitor Progress
- Data Collection

EFFECTIVE COMMUNICATION

EFFECTIVE COMMUNICATION can be achieved by focusing on activities based on purposeful language interactions. Purposeful talk is one of the major means through which children construct and refine their understandings of language. Talk should underpin all language activities.

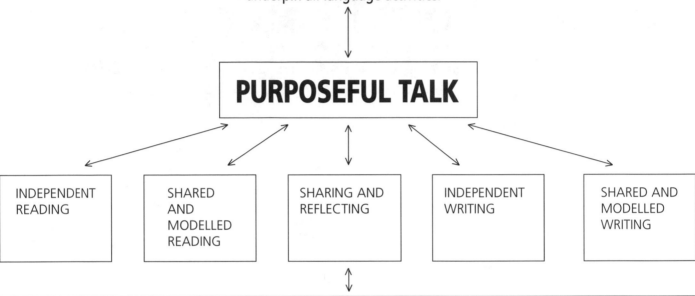

PURPOSEFUL TALK

| INDEPENDENT READING | SHARED AND MODELLED READING | SHARING AND REFLECTING | INDEPENDENT WRITING | SHARED AND MODELLED WRITING |

PURPOSEFUL TALK

Communication occurs when the speaker has effectively relayed his/her meaning to the listener.

Provide opportunities for:
- discussion across the curriculum;
- negotiation;
- group interaction;
- brainstorming;
- clarification of values and issues;
- reflective response to own and others' contributions;
- reading and retelling;
- storytelling;
- news telling;
- drama;
- reporting;
- debating and arguing;
- questioning and enquiring.

PURPOSEFUL WRITING

Communication occurs when the writer has effectively relayed his/her meaning to the reader.
Good spelling is a factor in effectively relaying meaning.

Provide opportunities for:
- learning about writing;
- learning through writing;
- analysing different forms in written context;
- modelled writing;
- editing;
- writing for different purposes and audiences; and
- self evaluation of writing development.

Encourage children to develop spelling skills through:
- word study activities, e.g. derivations, origins, morphemic units;
- visual patterning activities;
- identifying critical features of words;
- using spelling resources;
- word sorting;
- use of personal lists;
- proof reading;
- a range of strategies.

PURPOSEFUL READING

Effective communication occurs when a reader creates, interprets and analyses meanings from text.

Provide opportunities for:
- reading for a wide range of purposes;
- reading a wide variety of different text-types;
- critical reflection on and response to texts;
- discussion which encompasses different interpretations of and responses to text.

What Do We Know About Reading?

The Reading Developmental Continuum is built on the following beliefs about reading.

Beliefs about Reading

- The central purpose of reading is to gain meaning from print.
- Reading involves the integration of the cuing systems of language.
- Reading is an active process of constructing meaning.
- Readers bring a range of experiences, background knowledge and feelings to the text.
- Reading development is a continuous process throughout life.
- Reading strategies are important for the construction of meaning.

Beliefs about Learning to Read

- Children learn to read by being active in the process of controlling language.
- Reading should have significance for all children, they should understand the purposes for reading.
- Reading requires a knowledge of the linguistic system.
- Reading requires children to become responsible for applying skills and strategies.
- Children learn through immersion when they are exposed to demonstrations of how language is used in many varied situations.
- Skills and strategies are learnt in the context of whole language activities.

Beliefs about Reading Instruction

Teachers:
- establish a language-rich environment where print is presented in natural and meaningful contexts
- read to children every day from a range of literature that extends children's literary experiences
- present children with a wide range of reading materials
- ensure children have the opportunity to read independently every day
- provide opportunities for individual conferences where children discuss aspects of their reading
- model and discuss reading strategies, i.e. meaning making strategies, word identification and general strategies
- teach children how to monitor the effectiveness of reading strategies

- encourage children to respond to, and reflect on texts critically
- encourage children to take risks while making meaning
- emphasise strengths rather than weaknesses.

Desirable Outcomes of a Language Program

The reader:
- is self-motivated to read for pleasure or to satisfy a purpose
- sees books as a major source of information
- is confident and efficient in his/her control of and use of appropriate reading strategies
- is able to select, use, monitor and reflect on appropriate strategies for different reading purposes, e.g. pleasure, research, information
- uses reading to enter worlds beyond personal experience
- responds sensitively and perceptively to literature
- can identify likes and dislikes about different authors and justify opinions
- can reflect on, and respond to texts critically, providing different levels of interpretation and points of view
- can recognise and describe purpose and structure of different genres
- can read a text to find the main idea and key information
- can formulate and apply research skills using different texts.

How to Use the Reading Developmental Continuum

- **Predict** where the children are on the Continuum by looking at the Key Indicators
- **Collect Data** to confirm the prediction, through observation and collection of work samples
- **Involve** parents and children
- **Link Assessment with Teaching** by referring to the major teaching emphases
- **Monitor Progress** through ongoing collection of data, consultation with parents and linking children's current phase of development with teaching

Predict

- Read through the Overview of the Reading Developmental Continuum, with special reference to the Phase Descriptions and Key Indicators.
- Match your knowledge of the children in your class with the Phase Descriptions and Key Indicators to predict which phase each child is in. Experience shows that it takes about thirty seconds to place a child on the Continuum in this way.

Collect Data

The Continuum indicators will help you gather information about children's reading behaviours. Further information about collecting data is provided on page 18.

Place Children on the Continuum

- If children are exhibiting *any* of the indicators of the Role-Play Reading Phase, they are said to be operating in that phase.
- Beyond the Role-Play Phase, children who are exhibiting all the Key Indicators of a phase are said to be operating in that phase. If they are not yet exhibiting all the Key Indicators of a phase they are said to be operating in the phase before.
- For most of the children in a class, it is only necessary to look at the Key Indicators.
- If you choose to look at more than the Key Indicators you will expect and find that children may display behaviours across two or three phases. It is the Key Indicators, however, that are used to determine which phase children are operating in. This information is designed to inform and guide the teaching program.

- For children who are at risk and are experiencing difficulties teachers may wish to look at *all* the indicators because:
  - the complete range of indicators comprises a sensitive and fine-grained diagnostic tool that enables teachers to focus on children's current understandings and the strategies they are using. The information obtained provides insights into children's thinking and an individualised guide to teaching
  - it is sometimes difficult to measure the progress of children at risk, and it may appear that they are making little or no progress. It is encouraging for teachers, parents and the children themselves to be aware of the tiny but crucial gains that are actually being made
  - it is sometimes tempting to talk about children at risk in terms of what they *cannot* do. A focus on the achievement of behavioural indicators leads to a celebration of what children *can* do and an accurate assessment of how much they are learning.
- If a class contains several children at risk, it is suggested that only one of these children is observed for at least two weeks before concentrating on the next child.

Involve Parents and Children

Parents often have a very clear sense of their children's competencies. They are usually pleased to be asked to comment on what they have observed at home. Including parents in the assessment and monitoring process by asking for their observations may help you to gain an extremely accurate picture of the children.

Children are also keenly interested in their own progress and enjoy using the check list for children entitled *Things I*

Can Do. Experience has shown that very often children are their own harshest critics.

Once parents can see where their children are on the Continuum they will be interested in reading the pages of ideas that suggest how they may be able to further support their children's development at home.

Link Assessment With Teaching

When children are placed in phases, the section entitled Major Teaching Emphases will guide the selection of appropriate teaching strategies and activities. Many of these are described in some detail in this book. Others are discussed in the accompanying *First Steps Reading: Resource Book*. The key teaching strategies described in each phase are considered to be critical for children's further development. They can be used to meet the needs of a whole class, small groups and individual children.

Monitor Progress

The Developmental Continuum provides a sensitive and accurate means by which progress can be monitored over time. This involves further observation and data collection. Links are constantly made between assessment and teaching.

The reading record forms may be used to map individual or class progress. If entries are dated it is easy to see how a child is progressing. The record forms may also be used as a basis for reporting to parents.

Many schools synthesise class records twice a year to monitor overall progress and to inform the allocation of resources and support.

Data Collection

The purpose of evaluation is to identify how children are progressing and determine what support is needed. Teachers need to gather information about children's strengths and weaknesses and then plan appropriate teaching strategies to support further development. Evaluation should occur as a natural, ongoing part of the class program. Information about children's reading development should be gathered across a range of reading activities where children are working in different contexts with varied texts. Observations need to be systematic, informed and ongoing.

Data can be collected about the:

- understanding of ideas presented
- identification of important information in text
- ability to reflect on, and respond to texts critically, providing different levels of interpretation and points of view
- recognition of purpose and structure of different genres
- knowledge of personal reading strategies
- development of self-monitoring strategies
- application of appropriate strategies for different reading purposes, e.g. scanning to locate information, skimming for a general understanding
- extent to which the student's reading is reflected in their own writing
- interest in reading
- enjoyment of reading
- time spent reading
- willingness to pursue an author or topic
- confidence when reading different texts
- selection of reading material
- personal reading preferences
- range of genres read.

Ways of Gathering Data

- Oral or written retelling following silent reading
- Observing reading behaviours, e.g. selection of books, interest in reading tasks
- Observations during 'Directed Silent Reading', e.g. sub-vocalisation, finger pointing, use of picture cues
- Teacher questioning about a text
- Teacher-child conference
- Written retelling following silent reading
- Children's self-evaluation comments
- Observing classroom reading activities, e.g. cloze passages, story maps
- Teacher/child interviews
- Oral reading and miscue analysis

Part III

Phases of Reading Development

By scanning the phase descriptions and key indicators on the overview sheet at the beginning of this book, teachers can place children in a phase of the Reading Continuum. Part III of this book provides details of each phase, including all indicators and a wide range of appropriate teaching strategies.

Each phase includes:

- indicators describing children's behaviours; key indicators are marked and written in bold print
- teaching notes
- descriptions of the major teaching emphases
- a list of behaviours to be encouraged
- specific teaching strategies and activities for each phase of development
- notes for parents

Role Play Reading

In this phase readers display reading-like behaviour as they reconstruct stories for themselves. They show a natural interest in books and the language of print.

The following comments represent understandings of children in this phase.

What is Reading?

Christina:	*'Writing.'*
Clayton:	*'You get to read stories and you get to learn.'*
Annie:	*'When you turn the pages and you talk.'*
Thomas:	*'Having a story.'*
Katie:	*'For writing names.'*
James:	*'Reading a book.'*
Harry:	*'You gotta read before you go to school, '*
Mark:	*'Reading a book.'*

How do you read?

Bevan:	*'You turn the pages.'*
Clayton:	*'From the words.'*
Rhiannon:	*'From your eyes.'*
Christina:	*'Spelling…numbers.'*
James:	*'You read the letters when you're big.'*
Mark:	*'By copying the words.'*
Annie:	*'You look at the words and then you tell them.'*
Katie:	*'You get a book and read, you can't read with your hands.'*
Harry:	*'With your mouth.'*
Thomas:	*'I don't know - turn the pages over and turn them over some more.'*

Who reads?

Christina:	*'My mum.'*
Rhiannon:	*'Mummy and Daddy.'*
James:	*'My brother.'*
Katie:	*'Mothers, Doctors and lots of people.'*
Mark:	*'My brother.'*
Clayton:	*'My mum. Sometimes my mum and dad.'*
Annie:	*'Me, my big brother, my two big sisters.'*

Role Play Reading Indicators

Making Meaning at Text Level

The reader:

- ◆ **displays reading-like behaviour**
  - **holding the book the right way up**
  - **turning the pages appropriately**
  - **looking at words and pictures**
  - **using pictures to construct ideas**
- ◆ **realises that print carries a message but may read the writing differently each time, e.g. when 'reading' scribble to parents**
- ◆ **focuses on the meaning of a television program, story, or other text viewed, listened to or 'read'. Responses reflect understanding.**
- ◆ **makes links to own experience when listening to or 'reading' books, e.g. points to illustration, saying 'My dog jumps up too.'**
- • uses pictorial cues when sharing a book or 'reading', e.g. pointing to a picture in The Three Little Pigs, says 'The three little pigs left home.'
- • turns the pages of a book, telling the story from memory
- • knows that writing and drawing are different, e.g. 'Mummy reads the black bits.'
- • selects favourite books from a range, e.g. chooses a book saying, 'I want The Three Little Pigs.'
- • can talk about favourite stories and enjoys hearing them re-read
- • is beginning to use some book language appropriately, e.g. 'Once upon a time…' The child may use a 'reading' voice
- • responds to and uses simple terminology such as book, right way up, front, back, upside down.

Making Meaning Using Context

The reader:

- ◆ **uses pictorial and visual cues when watching television, listening to or 'reading' stories, i.e. talks about a television program, advertisement or picture in a magazine or book, relating it to own knowledge and experience**
- • reacts to environmental print, e.g. noticing a fast food sign the child says 'I want a hamburger.'

Making Meaning at Word Level

The reader:

- ◆ **recognises own name, or part of it, in print**
- • is beginning to recognise some letters, e.g. Sam says 'That's my name', pointing to 'Stop' sign.

Attitude

The reader:

- • displays curiosity about print by experimenting with 'writing' and drawing and asking 'What does that say?'
- • wants to look at books
- • offers to 'read' writing and points to text while 'reading', indicating the beginning of having-a-go
- • expresses enjoyment by joining in orally and responding emotively when listening to familiar stories
- • eagerly anticipates book-reading events that are part of daily routine.

Teaching Notes

Children in this phase have become aware of books and the joy that reading brings. They have begun to notice print in the environment. They display reading-like behaviours, holding the book the right way up and turning pages, but their reading at this stage is purely inventive. Children sit, turning the pages, either making up a story from the pictures or telling the story from memory. At this stage of development the child is unable to match written words to spoken words.

It is most important that children during this early stage of development frequently listen to adults reading. As they are listening to a story they are also learning other useful information about books and print. They learn that books are friends, books are fun. Their involvement with books and their love of stories leads them to want to hear them again and again. Through such repetition children come to understand that a story is the same each time it is read.

Children in this phase need to experience reading both at home and at school in a supportive and accepting environment. Their early attempts to read should meet with praise and encouragement.

Major Teaching Emphases

Making Meaning at Text Level
◆ **Encourage discussion and praise critical and divergent thinking**
◆ **Provide picture books with limited text that children can 'read' to themselves and others**
◆ **Reread favourite stories and rhymes**
◆ **Share 'big books' with children, incidentally modelling reading behaviours**
• Read to children every day and encourage children to 'read' the stories again themselves
• Select books that provide children with a wide range of literary experiences:
  – folk tales, which help children develop a sense of story and 'story language'
  – contemporary stories with links to children's lives
  – poetry
  – nursery rhymes and songs
• Expose children to a wide range of informational texts such as recipes, letters, books about insects, transport, sea creatures etc.
• Talk about books and authors' views of the world, comparing these with children's experiences and perceptions
• Encourage children to respond to stories by talking about how they might feel and telling what they would have done had they been characters in a story
• Encourage children to select books they want you to read

Making Meaning Using Context
◆ **Establish a language-rich environment, presenting print in natural and meaningful contexts**

◆ **Read from an enlarged text (big book) so that children can follow the print as it is read**
◆ **Read texts featuring rhyme, rhythm and repetition**
• In modelled and shared reading and writing sessions and incidentally during the day:
  – draw attention to features and meaning of functional print in the classroom and read it with the children
  – model and demonstrate directionality
  – relate spoken to written words in context
  – draw attention to relationships between words and pictures
• Read nursery rhymes, songs and jingles with the children which familiarise them with sounds and patterns of language

Making Meaning at Word Level

◆ **In modelled and shared reading and writing sessions and incidentally during the day:**
  – **show that a written word is a unit of print with space either side**
  – **talk about letters by name, relating initial letters to the sounds they represent**
  – **show that print is written left to right and top to bottom**
  – **relate spoken to written words in context**
  – **draw attention to relationships between words and pictures**
  – **demonstrate use of context cues to make meaning**
• Place a special focus on the letters of children's names and the sounds they represent
• Draw attention to long words, short words, unusual words and funny words
• Use children's names constantly to draw attention to the links between spoken and written language and the ways in which a word is represented in print.

At all phases:
◆ **foster children's enjoyment of reading, encouraging them to explore a variety of texts and take risks with confidence**
◆ **read to students every day and share your own enjoyment of reading**
◆ **encourage students to respond critically to texts they have read or viewed**
◆ **model reading behaviours and strategies for students to emulate**
◆ **encourage students to select their own books and read independently every day**
◆ **encourage students to share experiences related to reading and viewing**
◆ **talk to students about their reading and viewing**
◆ **provide opportunities for students to write every day for different purposes and audiences.**

◆ *Entries in bold are considered critical to the children's further development*

Behaviours to be Encouraged

Making Meaning at Text Level

- Responding to stories read, i.e. retelling, acting out, drawing, discussing, relating to own experience
- Using personal experience to construct meaning
- Predicting outcomes from text and picture cues
- Using context cues to construct meaning
- Using picture cues to construct meaning
- Adopting reading-like behaviours
- Attending to features and meanings of environmental print

Making Meaning Using Context

- Joining in with favourite parts of stories
- Recognising a known chunk of print in a very familiar story, e.g. 'The pig went wee, wee, wee, wee all the way home'
- Using pictures to support the text, e.g. 'The pig is running away.'

Making Meaning at Word Level

- Recognising own name
- Recognising initial letter or letters from own name in other words
- Recognising words from environmental print in context
- Recognising specific words in familiar books

Attitude

- Interacting with and enjoying literature through stories read by a teacher or adult
- Respecting and valuing books
- Asking questions about and commenting on print

Teaching Strategies

Making Meaning at Text Level

- Sensitise children to a wide range of literary language through reading varied materials.
- Select books that describe familiar experiences, concepts and objects.
- Make use of quality 'book and tape' sets so children can sit and listen to a story that is read well.
- Read nursery rhymes and simple poetry.
- Select books that play with language, nonsense words, rhyme and rhythm.
- Encourage children to discriminate between stories that interest them and those that don't.
- Encourage children to 'read' their own and other favourite stories to other children.
- Provide opportunities for children to select their own books.
- Encourage children to act out familiar rhymes, favourite stories or their own stories. Set up a puppet theatre and dress up corner.
- Read expressively bringing as much meaning to the language as possible.
- Model correct book handling techniques.
- Encourage children to predict what a story may be about after looking at the cover of the book.

- Discuss the illustrations.
- Encourage children to relate illustrations to their own experiences, e.g. point to picture and say, 'Is that bike like your bike?'
- Encourage children to retell stories from illustrations and from memory.
- Relate features of a story to the children's own experience, e.g. story about the beach—'You built a big sandcastle just like that one'.
- Select stories that children can relate to, asking them to predict words and phrases.
- Encourage children to talk about their drawing and writing.
- Set up an attractive reading corner where children's favourite books are always available.
- Encourage children to bring favourite books from home to share with the class.

Making Meaning Using Context.

- Select books with clear illustrations as support for the text. Focus attention on illustrations through questioning and comment.
- Write for different purposes in front of the children every day, e.g. leave a message for the cleaner, write a note to parents, write a letter or a thank-you card.
- Share letters, messages, birthday cards, thank-you cards, lists.
- Discuss conventions of print spontaneously during shared book reading by indicating:
  – title
  – front and back cover of book
  – the concept of a page
  – sentences as units of print
  – left to right progression along the line of print
  – top to bottom progression down the page.
- Read from an enlarged text (big book) so children can follow the print and join in spontaneously.
- Draw attention to environmental print through purposeful questioning, following instructions, modelled writing.
- Ask children to show where the story begins.
- Encourage children to use the illustrations to predict what might happen next.
- Write some messages to the children and respond in writing to any messages received from them.
- Talk about everyday print. Prepare charts of familiar community signs and discuss where these might be seen. Read packages and labels from the class shop.
- Take children on walks around their community pointing out and reading environmental print.
- Teach traditional rhymes and songs, chart these and read them together.

- Create a song box. As songs are taught, print them on cards for the children's use. Use pictures to assist children to recognise a song. During mat sessions encourage children to select, and 'read' or sing songs from the box. Use this idea for the storage of poems and rhymes as well.

- Transcribe children's oral language and make up class books for the children to 'read', e.g. Visit to the Zoo, Hatching chickens, Cooking fried rice.
- Read stories, poems, rhymes daily. It is especially helpful to read certain books several times and display them so children can talk their way through them.
- Involve the children in picture talks using pictures that show actions, familiar scenes and situations. Children may discuss the pictures with a partner, in groups or with the whole class. Write down what the children say and use the text for future reference.

Making Meaning at Word Level

- Select books that use repetition, rhyme and common language patterns.
- Encourage children to join in as stories are read from a shared book.
- Transcribe children's oral language for the purpose of teaching reading.
- Discuss concepts of print spontaneously during shared book reading by indicating:
  - words as units of print
  - letter names and sounds.
- Help children to recognise their own name (provide many opportunities for children to match and write their own name).
- Substitute character names in very familiar stories with names of children in the class.
- Encourage children to identify letters from their names during shared book sessions or while the teacher is scribing during modelled writing.
- Write captions under children's drawings as they dictate the text.

- Encourage children to 'write' their own captions on their drawings.
- Sometimes point to words as children read.
- Talk about words and letters, e.g. 'That's a long word isn't it? Let's count how many letters it has in it.'
- Involve the children in creating text for textless books.
- Write well-known nursery rhymes in front of children asking them to predict words and phrases.
- Scribe children's language:
  - to describe items of equipment
  - to describe children's constructions

  - to provide directions for using equipment
  - to describe group work.
- Use children's names to label belongings, pictures, shelves, coat pegs.
- Encourage children to talk about their drawing and writing.
- Share lists with children:
  - home shopping
  - centre shopping
  - children who are absent.
- Prepare wall stories. After children have been read or told a well-known story have them retell it. Then record four or five of the main sentences from the story. These can be printed on cards while children illustrate one of the ideas. Display children's illustrations above the appropriate sentence.

- Draw large pictures of characters from familiar nursery rhymes and fairy tales and attach speech bubbles or labels.

- Each week display a photo of a child from the class. Attach a speech bubble which explains what the child likes to do.

For Parents

How can I help my child with reading?

- Read to your child as often as you can.
- Encourage your child to choose the books you read together and help the child to tell the story from pictures in the book.
- Talk about the books you read and the people, things and animals in them.
- Draw attention to the illustrations when reading to your child.
- Enrol your child in the local library.
- Select books that describe familiar experiences, concepts and objects as well as fairy tales and fantasy stories.
- Make sure your child sees members of the family reading.
- Buy books as presents. Let your child help you choose them.
- Keep audio tapes of favourite stories and songs in the car to play on long journeys.
- Help your child to recognise his/her own name. Write simple dedications inside the child's own books and encourage them to start building their own book collection.
- Teach your child nursery rhymes and songs.
- Make use of quality 'book and tape' sets during busy times in the daily schedule.
- Select books that use repetition to capture the rhythm of language, e.g. *The Three Billy Goats Gruff*.
- Tell stories on the way to the shop, at bath time, at bed time.
- Always keep a selection of books in your bag.
- Place labels around the home, e.g. 'These are Kim's favourite books.'
- Hold the book so the child can see the pictures and writing.
- Let the child hold the book and turn the pages.
- Encourage the child to join in and 'read' too.
- Leave the book handy for private readings to teddy.
- Help your child to tell the story from the pictures in the book.
- Talk about everyday print, e.g. "We are going in here to get a hamburger. See the sign. it says 'Harry's Hamburgers'."
- Sometimes point to the words as you read.
- Talk about your plans, e.g. 'Today I am going to make a cake, let's look at the recipe.'

- Before beginning to read, settle your child down and talk a little about the book, e.g. 'This looks as if it's going to be a funny story.'
- Accept and praise your child's attempts to read.
- Visit the local book shop.
- Fill your child's room with posters, books, pictures, mobiles of book characters.
- Make a cloth book bag to take books with you wherever you go.

Experimental Reading

PHASE 2

In this phase readers use memory of familiar texts to match some spoken words and written words. They realise that print contains a constant message and begin pointing to words. They may comment on pictures, but seldom question written text.

The following comments represent understandings of children in this phase.

What is Reading?

Daniel: *'So you can learn what to do when you are about six.'*
Barry: *'It's words.'*
Dominique: *'I don't know.'*
Travis: *'It's something what you read. It's something what you look at and it's got words in.'*
Vita: *'I don't know.'*
Luke: *'Important.'*
Frank: *'To learn and reading for 'Mum'.'*
Robert: *'When you need words.'*

How do you Read?

Daniel: *'You look at the words constantly, that's all I know.'*
Barry: *'I just spell 'em out.'*
Dominique: *'My mum lets me.'*
Travis: *'You spell words out and then you ... read 'em.'*
Vita: *'You read by the words.'*
Luke: *'There's words there. You have to read them.'*
Frank: *'Look at the words and say the words.'*
Robert: *'When you have a book and there's pages with words in, then you read 'em.'*

Who Reads?

Daniel: *'I do.'*
Barry: *'We do.'*
Dominique: *'Me.'*
Travis: *'Teachers and little kids and Mums and Dads.'*
Vita: *'Everyone.'*
Luke: *'The person who's looking at the book.'*
Frank: *'Yourself. You need to do it yourself.'*
Robert: *'After school, when you put your signer in the bucket, and you take your book and your signer home, then you write in your signer that you read the book.'*

Experimental Reading Indicators

Making Meaning at Text Level

The reader:

- ◆ ~~realises that print contains a constant message, i.e. that the words of a written story remain the same, but the words of an oral story may change~~
- ◆ ~~is focused on expressing the meaning of a story rather than on reading words accurately~~
- knows that print goes from left to right and from top to bottom of a page
- responds to and uses terminology such as: letter, word, sentence, chapter
- is beginning to demonstrate awareness of literary language, e.g. 'a long, long time ago...', 'by the fire sat a cat', 'No, no, no', said the...'
- identifies the subject matter of a story through the use of titles and illustrations, e.g. 'I want the story about the big black cat'
- shows an ability to connect ideas and events from stories heard or viewed by retelling events in sequence, using pictures, memory of the story and knowledge of story structure
- expresses personal views about the actions of a character and speculates on own behaviour in a similar situation, e.g. 'If I had been...I would have...'
- sub-vocalises or whispers when reading 'silently'.

Making Meaning Using Context

The reader:

- ◆ **uses prior knowledge of context and personal experience to make meaning, e.g. uses memory of a text to match spoken with written words**
- demonstrates understanding of one-to-one correspondence between spoken and written words, for instance, the child slows down when dictating to an adult
- asks for assistance with some words. May be aware that own reading is not accurate and may seek help, re-read or stop reading
- uses patterns of language to predict words or phrases, e.g. repetitive refrains in shared book readings.

Making Meaning at Word Level

The reader:

- ◆ **recognises some personally significant words in context, e.g. in a job roster, weather chart or books**
- ◆ **matches some spoken words with written words when reading a book or environmental print**
- is developing the ability to separate a word from the object it represents. For instance, the child realises that

'Dad' is a little word, not that 'Dad' is a big word because Dad is big

- recognises some letters of the alphabet and is able to name them
- demonstrates some knowledge of letter-sound relationships, for instance, the sound represented by the initial and most salient letters in words
- points to specific known words as they are read
- uses initial letter sounds to predict words in texts.

Attitude:

The reader:

- is beginning to see self as a reader and talks about own reading
- may ask for favourite stories to be read
- joins in and acts out familiar stories if invited to do so
- selects books to read for pleasure
- self-selects texts on basis of interest or familiarity.

Teaching Notes

The experimental reader attempts to match knowledge of the text with print on the page. The reader is able to recognise some words and letters in context but still relies heavily on memory of the story, picture cues, prior knowledge of context and personal experience. As readers move through this phase they become increasingly tied to the print on the page and begin pointing to words and searching for key or familiar words.

Teachers need to continue to foster children's understanding and knowledge of concepts and conventions of print through activities which focus children's attention on print. Children need to understand that print contains a message, that the message is the same each time, that books are read in a certain way—front to back, top to bottom and from left to right along the line, and that written words match spoken words.

Children in this phase need the support of an adult to model effective reading strategies and help them as they become involved in meaningful reading activities.

Major Teaching Emphases

Making Meaning at Text Level

- ◆ **Share with children times when you challenge or disagree with a text**
- ◆ **Discuss instances of stereotyping in texts**
- ◆ **Value and encourage both critical and empathetic responses from children, especially those that are different from your own**
- ◆ **Before, during and after reading promote discussion that goes beyond the literal level**
- ◆ **Provide opportunities for children to retell stories**
- • Establish a language-rich environment, presenting print in natural and meaningful contexts
- • Read to children every day and encourage children to re-read stories and informational texts
- • Encourage children to select books which they wish to read or which they want you to read to them
- • Re-read old favourites
- • Select books that provide children with a wide range of literary experiences
  - – folk tales
  - – nursery rhymes
  - – contemporary stories
  - – picture books
  - – poetry
- • Expose children to a wide range of informational texts
- • Encourage children to respond to stories by talking about how they feel and what they might have done had they been a character in a story

Making Meaning Using Context

— setup store

◆ **Use environmental print purposefully each day**
◆ **Select reading material that is predictable, familiar and has natural repetition**
◆ **Discuss conventions of print informally when reading**
◆ **Model reading strategies such as predicting words and reading-on**
• Read from an enlarged text so that children can follow the print as you read
• Talk about repetitive phrases and sentences
• Model reading behaviours that children need to learn
• Provide opportunities for children to be involved in oral cloze activities using, for example, nursery rhymes, familiar big books and, language-experience texts

Making Meaning at Word Level

◆ **Involve students in oral cloze activities focusing on words**
◆ **Talk about letters and words in context, pointing out distinctive features**
◆ **Encourage children to explore letter–sound relationships**
• Write children's names in lists and label belongings, paintings etc.

At all phases:

◆ **foster children's enjoyment of reading, encouraging them to explore a variety of texts and take risks with confidence**
◆ **read to students every day and share your own enjoyment of reading**
◆ **encourage students to respond critically to texts they have read or viewed**
◆ **model reading behaviours and strategies for students to emulate**
◆ **encourage students to select their own books and read independently every day**
◆ **encourage students to share experiences related to reading and viewing**
◆ **talk to students about their reading and viewing**
◆ **provide opportunities for students to write every day for different purposes and audiences.**

◆ *Entries in bold are considered critical to the children's further development*

Behaviours to be Encouraged

Making Meaning at Text Level

- Using personal experience and previous interaction with similar or identical text
- Using knowledge of context and meaning
- Using knowledge of text structure, e.g. lists, greeting cards, story structure
- Using picture cues to make meaning

Making Meaning Using Context

- Using knowledge of oral language patterns
- Using rhyme, rhythm and repetition
- Using prediction
- Using syntactic knowledge, e.g. 'The jumping' sounds wrong and 'The dog is jumping' sounds right
- Using contextual and pictorial cues

Making Meaning at Word Level

- Using knowledge of concepts of print
- Attending to print by pointing to words read
- Attempting to decode words through:
  - noticing distinctive features of letters
  - noticing letter groupings and sounds
  - 'having a go' and taking risks
  - asking for assistance
  - recognising some words and letters in context

Attitude:

- Enjoying literature and so fostering good attitudes towards and participation in reading
- Imitating and inventing reading-like behaviours

Teaching Strategies

Making Meaning at Text Level

- Sensitise children to a wide range of literary language through reading varied materials.
- Select books that contain natural language that is easy to remember.
- Make use of quality 'book and tape' sets so that children can hear different interpretations of the print.
- Continue to read different types of texts in different contexts during the day, e.g. a letter or postcard, a message, a list, captions under pictures.
- Continue to read and write for different purposes in front of the children every day.
- Plan related activities after reading to help deepen and extend children's understanding, e.g. art, craft, cooking, writing.
- Read selections of stories that are related in some way, e.g. same author, structure, characters, style. Encourage children to make comparisons and explain similarities.
- Read part of a story to children then ask them to draw a picture of what they think will happen next.
- Help children to focus on the structure of a story, i.e. setting, character, events, complications, resolution.
- Provide opportunities for children to select their own books and read independently.
- Encourage children to talk about why they liked or disliked a particular book.
- Share with children the understanding that their view of the world may be different from that of the author's.
- Ask children to explain how they 'knew' answers to questions, i.e. comprehension strategies.
- Model enjoyment of books, express delight, surprise, anxiety.
- Make use of expression in voice to highlight different character traits.
- Encourage children to make predictions from the title.
- Encourage children to use the illustrations to predict what might happen next.
- Encourage children to identify the main idea of a story through use of the title and illustrations.
- Provide opportunities for children to retell stories from pictures and from memory.
- Provide opportunities for children to arrange pictures or text from a story in sequence, encouraging them to justify the logic of their sequence.
- Encourage children to make comparisons between stories.
- Encourage children to relate stories to personal experiences.
- Encourage children to agree/disagree with the author.

- Promote discussion before, during and after reading. Encourage children to predict what they think will happen or why something did or did not happen.
- Use questioning and discussion to encourage children to draw conclusions and make inferences.
- Involve children in discussions that encourage them to think beyond the literal level, e.g. 'Why do you think the troll lived under the bridge?'
- Provide children with the opportunity to respond to stories through drawing, drama or puppets.
- Encourage written responses after story time and display these in the reading corner.
- Develop a class diary or journal. Teacher writes collaboratively with the children about class activities. Children volunteer to illustrate pages.
- Develop a reading corner that is attractive to children. Include new books and books that are old favourites.

- Read to children daily from a variety of forms of text.
- Draw children's attention to narrative language when reading fiction, e.g. 'Once upon a time', 'happily ever after', 'a long, long time ago'.
- Continue reading books of rhymes, poetry and riddles and give children their own copies of songs they are learning.
- Retell favourite stories, poems and rhymes using felt board or overhead projector.
- Encourage children to bring photographs of themselves along to school and then dictate a caption for photograph. Photographs and captions can then be displayed. If children do not have photographs, use drawings.
- Use picture books to develop understanding of narratives, e.g. Teacher reads picture book to the class and then individuals retell the story. This could be a one-to-one exercise, a small group activity of individual retelling onto a tape.
- Tell a story to the class and then encourage children to tell this story to someone at home in exchange for another story. The children then retell the exchanged story at school to teacher, friend or class.

Making Meaning Using Context

- Select books that contain an abundance of cues on which to base predictions and confirmation.
- Select books which use repetitive structure so children can depend on the language of the book to make sensible predictions.
- Select books where pictures support the text. This is important for prediction and confirmation.
- Select books that use familiar oral language patterns so children are able to match these with the oral language patterns they know.
- Encourage children to join in as stories are read during shared reading sessions.
- Ask children to match sentences to class labels around the room.
- Tape individual children's talk and transcribe it. Encourage the child to read it back. Praise attempts to match taped talk with the print.
- Continue to transcribe children's oral language for the purpose of teaching reading, e.g. use the text for:
  – sequencing activities
  – cloze activities.
- Read from enlarged text (big book) so children can follow the print and join in spontaneously.
- Encourage children to write their own stories/messages and read them to others.
- Make up wall charts of the text from an entire book so the children are able to see all the text at once. This is useful for text innovation and helps the children recognise rhyme and rhythmic patterns.
- Ask children to point out something they noticed during shared reading of a book, e.g. repetition, letter of own name, interesting words.
- Model specific reading strategies, e.g. 'Oh, I have lost my place. I will just re-read this page.'
- Display a recipe written in large print on a chart during cooking activities so children can follow as you read.

- Involve the children in 'treasure hunts' where clues have to be read to find out where to go next.

- Involve children in cloze activities during shared book sessions. At first omit only about one word in twenty, choosing verbs. Then move on to omitting some nouns along with verbs. Always leave the first sentence intact. Encourage the children to think of a meaningful replacement, e.g. 'What will the next word be? Does it make sense; does it sound right?'.

- Provide opportunities for children to substitute rhyming words. Focus attention on particular words in a story, nursery rhyme or poem. Ask children to suggest alternative rhyming words. Tape new words over the old words and have the children read their new version.
- Provide opportunities for children to write every day, always having-a-go at spelling the words they want.
- Encourage children to make up stories from textless picture books.
- Have children draw and write every day and talk about their drawings, writing and favourite stories.
- Develop the concept of 'left to right'. Stick a coloured dot on the left hand top corner of their desk to act as a reminder. Children suggest where the teacher should start when transcribing stories.
- Read books that 'play with language patterns', e.g. 'Dr Seuss' books.
- Involve children in chanting:
  – favourite poems and rhymes
  – health and safety poems
  – frame sentences.
- Write story parts on cards and introduce these with the pictures. Children can use the cards for sequencing and retelling activities. Encourage children to 'read' along with repetitive sentences, e.g. 'Who's going trip, trap over my bridge?' Ensure these pictures and cards are easily accessible to the children.
- Make 'big books' with the children using simple repetitive texts. Include children's drawings, photographs and names.
- Develop 'Our Class Riddle' book. Children write out their favourite riddles or make up their own. Riddles can be used to introduce children to cloze activities.

Making Meaning at Word Level

- Ask children to match words in the text to words in the environment.
- Ask children to match names to class helpers charts.

- Write children's news and then ask children to identify any words beginning with 'Mm' etc. Children volunteer other words which begin with the same sounds and/or the same letters.
- Develop activities from blackboard or charted stories, e.g. 'What is the sound of 'S' in these words? sit, ship, his, dress?'
- Read tongue twisters to children encouraging them to focus on letter-sound relationships.
- Transcribe children's oral language and use it to teach:
  - development of sight word vocabulary
  - letter matching games.
- Develop cloze activities from familiar texts by covering parts of words leaving graphophonic cues, e.g. Mary st___ on a sharp rock. Her foot would not stop bl___.
- Encourage children to predict words in text by looking at the beginning letters in a word. Model this strategy.
- Develop class alphabet word banks. Ask the children to collect words beginning with a particular letter.

- Involve children in sorting words in different ways, e.g. visual patterns, sound patterns and meaning based relationships (Word Sorting):
  - sort the 'bl' words from the 'gr' words
  - sort out any words with an 'h' in them
  - sort out all the words with an 'e' sound in them
  - sort out all words with the word 'the' in them.

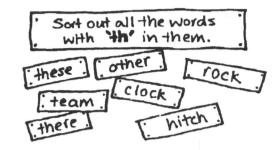

- Provide opportunities for children to find small words in large words.
- Make use of familiar text for:
  - word matching games
  - letter matching games.
- Provide opportunities for children to develop personal word banks of sight words, class focus words, interesting words.

- Encourage children to label their work with their names—provide name cards on their tables.
- Let children experiment with writing names in fingerpaint, sand, water on concrete, clay, play dough, plastic letters, pipe cleaners.
- Draw attention to sound-symbol relationships always in the context of text experiences.

For Parents

How can I help my child with reading?

- Read to your child whenever you can. Now and again ask a few 'why' questions about the story as you read.
- Help your child to tell stories from pictures in the book.
- Talk about the characters, plots and settings of stories.
- Discuss information gleaned from factual books.
- Enrol your child in the local library. Choose books together.
- Talk about reading the newspaper, magazines and books.
- Encourage your child to try and write his/her own name in books he/she owns.
- Read books of children's poetry with your child.
- Borrow 'book and tape' sets from the library.
- Compare events and people in books with your own lives.
- Talk about the pictures when reading to your child.
- Tell stories and sing songs in the car, at bath time, at bed time.
- Take books with you when visiting.
- Draw attention to print on packages, jars, e.g. 'Here is the Readybrek. This says, *Readybrek*.'. Point to print.
- Let your child 'read' to you, or to the cat.
- Encourage the child to join in when reading familiar stories.
- Talk about everyday print. Discuss advertisements and talk about the effect they have on you.

- Point out interesting or long words in books.
- Accept your child's efforts without criticism. Always encourage and praise his or her efforts.
- Print your child's name while the child watches when labelling lunch box etc.
- Read birthday cards with your child, pointing to the words.
- Write shopping lists in front of your child and talk about what you are doing.
- Set up a home message board and write a message everyday, e.g. 'Today we are going to grandma's.'
- Leave plenty of scrap paper, pencils and crayons on the child's table or desk. Give him/her old diaries or inexpensive notebooks.
- Encourage your child to write messages for different family members.
- Encourage your child to find words that begin with the same letter as his/her name.
- Recognise letters on car numberplates.
- Watch and talk about television with your child.
- Encourage your child to look at the title and cover of a book and guess what it may be about.
- Encourage your child to tell the story from the pictures in the book.

Early Reading

In this phase readers may read slowly and deliberately as they focus on reading exactly what is on the page. Unfamiliar texts may be read word-by-word. As word recognition increases, a wider range of text structures using familiar vocabulary can be read. Readers are beginning to reflect on their own strategies, e.g. for working out unknown words. They are beginning to realise that it is good to comment on and sometimes question texts they have read or listened to.

The following comments represent understandings of children in this phase.

What is Reading?

Emma: *'Things that I like to read about and everything.'*
Nicola: *'Something that you read when you go to bed or something like that.'*
Kerren: *'Read a book.'*
Alex: *'Read something.'*
Peter: *'It's when you get a book and you read it, what's inside it.'*
Stacey: *'Things that you read.'*
Jeremy: *'About you read books and that.'*
David: *'Looking at words.'*
Leima: *'You have to do some work.'*
Michael: *'Writing.'*
Philip: *'You read. It's good for you.'*

How do you read?

Emma: *'You read by words.'*
Nicola: *'You get a book and read the words. It's easy.'*
Kerren: *'When you talk you can read.'*
Alex: *'Read the words.'*
Peter: *'By going to school.'*
Stacey: *'By sounding the letters, if you can't read it.'*
Jeremy: *'By sounding out the letters.'*
David: *'Learning.'*
Leima: *'You have to read like this. You get one of the books and do your reading and make beautiful pictures.'*
Michael: *'Talk.'*
Philip: *'By learning at school.'*

Who reads?

Emma: *'We do. I do.'*
Nicola: *'People.'*
Kerren: *'Me.'*
Alex: *'Anybody.'*
Peter: *'The teacher.'*
Stacey: *'Me.'*
Jeremy: *'I do.'*
David: *'The teacher.'*
Leima: *'The teacher.'*
Michael: *'Me.'*
Philip: *'Us. Everybody.'*

Early Reading Indicators

Making Meaning at Text Level

The reader:

◆ **is beginning to read familiar texts confidently and can retell major content from visual and printed texts, e.g. language experience recounts, shared books, simple informational texts and children's television programs**

◆ **can identify and talk about a range of different text forms such as letters, lists, recipes, stories, newspaper and magazine articles, television dramas and documentaries**

◆ **demonstrates understanding that all texts, both narrative and informational, are written by authors who are expressing their own ideas**

- identifies the main topic of a story or informational text and supplies some supporting information
- talks about characters in books using picture clues, personal experience and the text to make inferences
- provides detail about characters, setting and events when retelling a story
- talks about ideas and information from informational texts, making links to own knowledge
- has strong personal reaction to advertisements, ideas and information from visual and written texts
- makes comparisons with other texts read or viewed. The reader's comments could relate to theme, setting, character, plot, structure, information or the way the text is written
- can talk about how to predict text content, e.g. 'I knew that book hadn't got facts in it. The dinosaurs had clothes on.'

Making Meaning Using Context

The reader:

◆ **may read word-by-word or line-by-line when reading an unfamiliar text, i.e. reading performance may be word centred. Fluency and expression become stilted as the child focuses on decoding**

◆ **uses picture cues and knowledge of context to check understanding of meaning**

- generally makes meaningful substitutions, however over-reliance on graphophonics may cause some meaning to be lost
- may sub-vocalise when reading difficult text 'silently'
- is beginning to use self-correction as a strategy
- uses knowledge of sentence structure and punctuation to help make meaning (syntactic strategies)
- sometimes reads-on to confirm meaning

- re-reads passage in order to clarify meaning that may have been lost due to word-by-word reading. May re-read a phrase, a sentence or a paragraph.
- can talk about strategies used at the sentence level, e.g. 'If I think it doesn't sound right, I try again.'
- is beginning to integrate prediction and substantiation.

Making Meaning at Word Level

The reader:

◆ **has a bank of words which are recognised when encountered in different contexts, e.g. in a book, on the blackboard, in the environment or on a chart**

◆ **relies heavily on beginning letters and sounding-out for word identification (graphophonic strategies)**

- carefully reads text, demonstrating the understanding that meaning is vested in the words
- may point as an aid to reading, using finger, eyes or voice, especially when reading difficult text
- locates words from sources such as Word Banks and environmental print
- when questioned can reflect on own word identification strategies, e.g. 'I sounded it out'.

Attitude

The reader:

- is willing to have-a-go at reading unknown words
- enjoys listening to stories
- reads for a range of purposes, e.g. for pleasure or information
- responds sensitively to stories read
- discusses favourite books
- talks about favourite author
- selects own reading material according to interest, purpose and level of difficulty and, with teacher support, can reconstruct information gained.

Teaching Notes

Readers in this phase may read slowly and deliberately as they focus on reading exactly what is on the page. As they become aware that print stays the same, more attention is paid to letters and sounds with some laboriously sounding out any word they are not sure of. While pictures are still useful in making meaning, more reliance is placed on the text itself with readers beginning to self-correct and re-read.

As in all phases, discussion will focus on meaning and the reader's reactions to the meaning that has been constructed.

Readers in this phase need to be made aware of the strategies that readers use when they don't know a word or when meaning isn't clear. It is important that teachers talk about and model these strategies during shared reading sessions. Readers should be encouraged to reflect on and discuss the strategies they are using.

Readers in this phase also need to be developing a basic sight vocabulary of high frequency words. Teachers should support this development by ensuring exposure to books that use these words in meaningful contexts.

Major Teaching Emphases

Making Meaning at Text Level

- ◆ **Ask readers about ideas and information they have found in books. Encourage a range of opinions and reactions, discuss stereotypes and generalisations.**
- ◆ **Provide opportunities for individual conferences where students discuss aspects of their reading**
- ◆ **Provide opportunities for students to demonstrate understanding of a text**
- ◆ **Encourage students to reflect on personal reading strategies**
- ◆ **Model strategies such as substituting, re-reading, and self-correcting during shared reading sessions**
- Establish a language-rich environment. Present print in natural and meaningful contexts
- Read to students every day and encourage them to re-read stories heard. Select books which provide students with a wide range of literary experiences.
- Ensure that students have the opportunity to select their own books to read independently every day
- Foster students' ability to predict through questioning and discussion before, during and after reading
- Encourage readers to share experiences related to their reading
- Read from an enlarged text (big book) and encourage students to join in
- Provide opportunities for readers to retell stories or impart information they have gained from books. Include stories and informational texts from whole class shared reading and independent reading.

Making Meaning Using Context

◆ **Encourage use of personal experiences, knowledge of oral language patterns and text structure to help readers make meaning**

• Provide opportunities for readers to demonstrate understanding of a text through activities such as:
  – substantiating answers by reading from the text
  – sequencing text
  – developing a story map
  – making comparisons with other texts
  – identifying the main idea of a story and providing some supporting information
  – identifying character traits

Making Meaning at Word Level

◆ **Model strategies for attacking unknown words, e.g. identifying similar word beginnings, common word patterns, chunking parts of a word**

◆ **Support the development of a basic sight vocabulary by:**
  – **selecting resources that use many of these words in a natural way**
  – **encouraging readers to re-read favourite books**
  – **scribing the students' own language in language experience stories and then using this text to focus on basic sight words**
  – **developing class word banks containing topic words, high frequency words, linking words etc.**

At all phases:

◆ **foster children's enjoyment of reading, encouraging them to explore a variety of texts and take risks with confidence**

◆ **read to students every day and share your own enjoyment of reading**

◆ **encourage students to respond critically to texts they have read or viewed**

◆ **model reading behaviours and strategies for students to emulate**

◆ **encourage students to select their own books and read independently every day**

◆ **encourage students to share experiences related to reading and viewing**

◆ **talk to students about their reading and viewing**

◆ **provide opportunities for students to write every day for different purposes and audiences.**

◆ *Entries in bold are considered critical to the children's further development*

Behaviours to be Encouraged

Making Meaning at Text Level

- Using personal knowledge and experience
- Using knowledge of text structure, e.g. structure of stories, letters, lists, recipes
- Using pictures to enhance meaning of text
- Using knowledge of conventions of print
- Responding to and reflecting on text meaning
- Using previous knowledge of stories or informational texts
- Using prediction combined with confirmation of text outcomes
- Critical thinking, questioning, commenting on content and intention
- Recognising important information in texts and identifying supporting detail
- Self-monitoring of reading strategies

Making Meaning Using Context

- Using knowledge of oral language patterns
- Using pictures and context to predict words
- Using rhyme, rhythm and repetition
- Re-reading and reading-on to re-establish meaning
- Sub-vocalising when unsure of text
- Using self-correction
- Using own knowledge and experience to create meaning

Making Meaning at Word Level

- Using knowledge of letters and visual letter patterns
- Sounding out
- Blending sounds and word parts
- Using knowledge of known sight words
- Locating words from word banks and environmental print

Attitude

- Having-a-go
- Discussing authors, stories and other texts
- Selecting own reading material
- Reading for a range of purposes
- Responding sensitively to stories

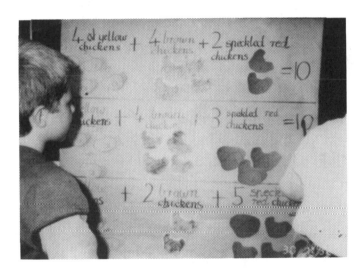

Teaching Strategies

Making Meaning at Text Level

- Begin each day by reading a 'big book' together. Discuss title, author, illustrator. Identify other books by the same author or on the same topic. Encourage children to look at the cover and make predictions about the content.
- Provide children with opportunities to select their own books for individual reading:
  - establish a process for conferencing children about their individualised reading
  - show children how to develop personal reading logs.
- Plan activities where children are reading for different purposes, e.g.
  - reading jokes and riddles to entertain
  - following instructions to make something
  - solving secret messages.
- Ensure that there is time for children to discuss the story they have read. Ask questions which focus on the author's craft, e.g.
  - Why do you think the author chose a particular word?
  - How do the illustrations help us understand the text?
- Encourage children to ask each other questions. Encourage children to talk about why they liked or didn't like a particular book.
- Encourage children to make comparisons with other texts. Read selections of stories or poems that are related to some way, e.g. same author, form, character, style. Encourage children to make comparisons or explain similarities.
- Talk about roles, assumptions and stereotypes. Encourage critical thinking.
- Model story mapping for the children. Teachers 'think aloud' as they explain the process. Show children various examples of 'maps' of familiar stories encouraging them to identify particular features. Children then develop their own maps of a familiar story. These may be used to support them when retelling the story.

- Discuss the use of speech bubbles during shared reading. Model the writing of speech bubbles during modelled writing. Use speech bubble activities, e.g.

children complete a speech bubble for a particular character to show what the character might have said before, during or after a particular event in a story.
- Use cooking activities for reading and writing purposes, e.g. the children read the recipe, carrying out instructions and then write about the experience.
- Read and discuss non-fiction texts. Help children identify particular features of this form and understand its purpose, e.g. contents page, index, glossary labels, keys, bibliography. Discuss what is in the text and what has been left out.
- Help children to understand how photographs, illustrations and diagrams are used in non-fiction texts.
- Involve the children in making their own fiction and non-fiction class books, e.g. 'Our Guinea Pigs', 'The Magic Xylophone'.
- Model the use of a simple semantic map to record particular features of a text.
- Prepare children for 'Readers Theatre' by orchestrating simple class poems and stories. Plan for whole class involvement, with parts for individuals, small groups and whole class. The children read parts from the text, they are not asked to memorise parts.

```
READERS' THEATRE
Narrator: Once upon a time there lived a
dear little girl. Her name was
Red Riding Hood. One day her
mother said:
Mother: 'Red Riding Hood, I want you to
visit your Grandmother. Take her
this basket of food.'
```

- After reading a story ask children to draw a picture of their favourite scene and then retell the story beginning from the part that happened before their picture.
- Encourage children to share and display their favourite sentences from literature they have read.

- Encourage children to share experiences related to their reading. Find other books related to the topic. Promote discussions before, during and after reading.
- Encourage children to use the illustrations to:
  - predict what may happen next
  - make inferences about character traits
  - identify supporting detail.
- Develop knowledge of text structure, e.g. repetitive sequence (*Billy Goats Gruff*), cumulative sequence (*This is the House that Jack Built*), chronological sequence (*The Three Bears*). Collect and categorise favourite stories and poems.
- Focus on text structure through:
  - comparing several narratives
  - developing story maps
  - modelling different forms of writing for the children
  - having the children identify 'rules' for writing different forms

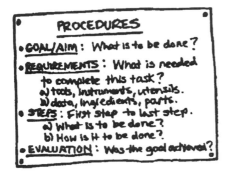

- Provide opportunities for children to retell stories from pictures and from memory.
- Have children sequence chunks of text and then discuss their arrangement.
- Ask children to identify all that they *know* about a topic and then generate a list of things that they would like to know before reading a non-fiction text.
- In shared book sessions focus on:
  - reading as a writer—developing concepts of authorship
  - appreciating style of writing
  - use of conventions in written language
  - developing a sense of story.
- Develop a class diary. Each day a child draws a picture and writes an appropriate sentence. Display pictures and sentences building up a record of the months' events.
- Invite authors to come and talk to the children about writing books. Ask them to talk about the process they went through, from initial planning to publishing.
- Plan language experience activities that require all children to participate actively in talking, reading and writing for real purposes, e.g.
  - making a cake
  - making a kite
  - planning a birthday party
  - making up a game.

- Organise excursions to further enhance the learning/teaching situation. Involve children in:
  - making plans
  - writing letters
  - planning questions
  - carrying out research.
- Provide activities to follow shared experiences, e.g.
  - writing stories or poems
  - making a wall story
  - writing captions for a mural
  - making an individual, group or class book
  - making a class chart
  - recording their experience on tape
  - make an overhead projector transparency about their experience.
- Allow time for children to talk about favourite books and read out parts of stories, poems and riddles they have enjoyed. This may be suggested to children as an alternative to 'newstelling'.
- Allow time during the day for a 'DEAR' (Drop Everything and Read) session.
- Provide opportunities for children to take part in circle stories. In this activity a child begins a story, this can be a retell or an original tale and then passes the 'storystick' on to the next child who continues the tale and so it goes on. This idea can be carried over to writing where children write the beginning of a story and pass it on for another child to continue. A lot of discussion will be generated as to the outcome of the story in relation to the initial idea.
- Ensure that purposeful reading becomes an important part of school assemblies, e.g.
  - children read out stories, poems, or reports they have written
  - children perform 'Readers Theatre'
  - children read out summaries of class events
  - children share language experience stories
  - children review new books from the school library.

Making Meaning Using Context

- Provide opportunities for children to manipulate and sequence words, phrases and sentences, after reading a text. Include such activities as:
  - reordering words, phrases, sentences
  - arranging sentences from a text in a logical order and then justifying choices made
  - completing a prepared cloze on the text
  - using a repetitive phrase from the text to develop own text.
- Use quality 'audio tape and book' sets to support children who are struggling with reading, the child can read along with the tape, joining in whenever he/she knows the word. The child is encouraged to read the book to the teacher when the child feels he/she is ready.

- Use text innovation to enhance children's control over text, e.g. select a favourite song, poem or shared book, cover appropriate words and ask the children to suggest other words that would make sense. Read through the 'new' version of the song, poem or story.
- Draw attention to the use of literary devices during shared reading sessions, e.g. rhyme, repetition, alliteration and onomatopoeia. Develop a group poem with the class. Take a refrain like 'Be quiet be quiet' and ask each child to suggest a one line statement. Record these on the blackboard putting in the refrain after every three or four lines. In this way you build up a really interesting whole class 'poem'.
- Model use of environmental print by using print around the room to focus on particular aspects of language
- Encourage children to read-on when they are not sure of a word. Model strategies such as substituting a particular word for the unknown word and read-on. Children are encouraged to return to the unknown word when they have completed the passage.
- Encourage children to re-read when they have lost meaning or become confused over an unknown word. Model re-reading during shared book sessions.
- Allow time for children to self-correct. Avoid stopping the child as soon as she/he makes a mistake.
- Model both primary and secondary word-solving strategies, i.e. in the context of shared reading experiences.
  Use of context and semantic cues:
  - delete words that encourage children to use the semantic knowledge to predict
  - underline words in context and ask children to explain the meaning
  - insert a nonsense word into a sentence and encourage children to find the appropriate word to replace it.
- Ensure children are reading for different purposes across the different curriculum areas, e.g.
  - reading for enjoyment
  - reading for specific information
  - reading to extract and organise information, e.g. reading for research purposes
  - reading to follow instructions.

Making Meaning at Word Level

- Use cloze activities to focus on different aspects of language, e.g. to focus on developing knowledge of basic sight words, delete sight words from a piece of text and place at the top of the page. Children complete the cloze by selecting the appropriate word for the space.

- Use shared book experiences to focus on words. After the children are familiar with the text, focus on sound-symbol relationships noticed by the children, e.g. double letters, initial sounds of words, word endings, rhyming words, different letters or letter clusters. Develop charts recording these 'discoveries'. The children are encouraged to add to the chart when they find other words belonging to a particular group.

- In shared reading sessions model the use of secondary word identification strategies:
  - give children groups of letters and ask them to see how many words they can make
  - take a word from a familiar text and ask children how many smaller words they can make out of it, first using the letters in order, then in any order
  - ask children to think of words to rhyme with a given word
  - complete a cloze activity with word endings omitted
  - categorise and classify words according to particular spelling patterns.
- Ask children to find words in text with particular letter patterns.
- Model focusing on the beginning of a word to aid word identification.
- Encourage children to reflect on own strategies, e.g. for working out unknown words.
- Encourage children to identify recurring patterns of letters in words, e.g. 'bridge - that looks a bit like branch'.
- Develop children's awareness of conventional spelling and common English letter patterns in the context of 'Shared Book'. Focus on:
  - common English letter patterns in words
  - short words within longer words
  - words that look similar
  - rhyming words
  - word endings.

For Parents

How can I help my child with reading?

- Continue to read to your child every day. Vary the type of books read, e.g. short stories, poems or serialise long stories.
- When reading to your child stop sometimes and ask 'What do you think might happen next?' Accept the child's answers even though they may not seem right.
- Occasionally ask some 'why' questions about the story, e.g. 'Why do you think the author put that bit in the story?'
- Talk about books your child has read at school.
- Take your child to the local library regularly and to any story telling sessions that are advertised.
- Buy books as presents to commemorate special occasions.
- Talk about the things you read — newspapers, magazines, books etc.
- Browse together in bookshops.
- Talk about books you are reading together. Compare characters with real people.
- Accept your child's efforts with praise, concentrate on all the things he/she does right, not on the few errors.
- Have plenty of scrap paper, pencils, felt pens and crayons on the child's table or desk. Give a diary, birthday book or notebook for Christmas.
- Talk about illustrations to see if they match what is in the child's or your mind.
- Leave notes around the house or under your child's pillow.
- Point out the author's name before reading a book and encourage your child to read other books by that author.
- If your child makes a mistake when he or she is reading aloud, allow time for self-correction. If the mistake makes sense, ignore it.
- Encourage your child to write messages to other family members.
- Encourage your child to write letters, postcards, lists, messages. Accept spelling mistakes.
- Encourage your child to make birthday, Christmas and Easter cards, party invitations. Children can write their own greetings and verses.
- Buy your child games that provide simple instructions to read and follow. Play word games.
- Look at the TV guide together and choose a program to watch.

- Encourage your child to make up plays for the family, acting out stories. Some children like to write simple scripts and to draw up a plan for other children to follow.
- Share letters and postcards from friends with the whole family.
- Encourage your child to keep a diary or journal when you go on holidays. This is particularly valuable if you are travelling and your child is missing school.
- Play numberplate games in the car, e.g. 'silly sentences' - FCF could be 'Fat Cows Flying'.
- Encourage children to retell stories. Involve the family in swapping stories, e.g. 'I'll tell you a story if you tell me one.'

Transitional Reading

PHASE 4

In this phase readers are beginning to integrate a range of reading strategies to make meaning. They are becoming more confident in using a variety of strategies to identify and comprehend words. They are able to adapt their reading to different types of text. Readers in this phase enjoy challenges, e.g. 'I'm going to read this hard book. I like lots of hard words.' Although books may influence their thinking, they may not be consciously aware of this. With teacher support they will comment on and criticise texts.

The following comments represent understandings of children in this phase.

What is Reading?

Nicole: *'Reading is writing, writing is what I am doing now.'*
Marcia: *'Reading is what you do when you've got a book.'*
Lisa: *'Reading is eyes seeing paragraphs of words.'*
Valerie: *'Looking at words and understanding what a person is trying to say.'*
Andrew: *'Reading is a bunch of words that have been put together to make a book, a story.'*
Albert: *'Something printed on a piece of paper.'*
Amanda: *'Reading is what your eyes and your brain tell you to see.'*
Michael: *'Looking at words and understanding them.'*

How do you Read?

Nicole: *'You read with your eyes.'*
Marcia: *'You read with a book that has words and your eyes.'*
Lisa: *'You read by moving your eyes side to side and up and down.'*
Valerie: *'You look at the letters and when you put them together they form a word.'*
Andrew: *'You read with your eyes but you can't really read unless you can spell.'*
Albert: *'By looking at the words on the piece of paper.'*
Amanda: *'I read differently to other people because I read slowly.'*
Michael: *'By looking at a piece of paper with words on.'*

Who Reads?

Nicole: *'Everyone reads at one stage of life.'*
Marcia: *'Sometimes people read when they're bored or they have nothing to do.'*
Lisa: *'People read.'*
Valerie: *'People read because they are unhappy or just for the fun of it or for learning purposes.'*
Andrew: *'People including me.'*
Albert: *'People who receive letters and bills and by reading books.'*
Amanda: *'People except for blind people because they're blind but they read differently to us.'*
Michael: *'Mum, Dad, Scott, me. Blind people read braille. Lots of people read.'*

Transitional Reading Indicators

Making Meaning at Whole Text Level

The reader:

◆ **shows an ability to construct meaning by integrating knowledge of:**
  - **text structure, e.g. letter, narrative, report, recount, procedure**
  - **text organisation, e.g. paragraphs, chapters, introduction, conclusion, contents page, index**
  - **language features, e.g. descriptive language, connectives such as because, therefore, if…then**
  - **subject specific language, e.g. the language of reporting in science and the language of a journalistic report**
◆ **can retell and discuss own interpretation of texts read or viewed with others, providing information relating to plot and characterisation in narrative or to main ideas and supporting detail in informational text**
◆ **recognises that characters can be stereotyped in a text, e.g. a mother looking after children at home while the father goes out to work or a prince rescuing a helpless maiden from an evil stepmother, and discusses how this could be changed**
◆ **selects appropriate material and adjusts reading strategies for different texts and different purposes, e.g. skimming to search for a specific fact; scanning for a key word**
- makes inferences and predictions based on information which is both explicit and implicit in a text
- makes generalisations based on interpretation of texts viewed or read, i.e. confirms, extends, or amends own knowledge through reading or viewing
- uses a range of strategies effectively to find relevant information in texts, e.g. makes use of table of contents and index
- reads orally with increasing fluency and expression. Oral reading reflects personal interpretation
- makes comparisons with other texts read
- selects texts effectively, integrating reading purpose and level of difficulty
- recognises devices which influence construction of meaning, such as the attribution of 'good' or 'bad' facial characteristics, clothing or language; and the provision of emotive music and colour; and stereotypical roles and situations in written or visual texts.

Making Meaning Using Context

The reader:

◆ **is becoming efficient in using most of the following strategies for constructing meaning:**
  - **makes predictions and is able to substantiate them**
  - **self-corrects when reading**
  - **re-reads to clarify meaning**
  - **reads-on when encountering a difficult text**
  - **slows down when reading difficult texts**
  - **substitutes familiar words**
  - **uses knowledge of print conventions, e.g. capitalisation, full stops, commas, exclamation marks, speech marks**
◆ **makes meaningful substitutions, i.e. replacement miscues are meaningful, e.g. 'cool' drink for 'cold' drink. The integration of the three cuing systems (semantic, syntactic and graphophonic) is developing**
- is able to talk about some of the strategies for making meaning.

Making Meaning at Word Level

The reader:

◆ **has an increasing bank of sight words, including some difficult and subject-specific words, e.g. science, experiment, February, Christmas**
◆ **is becoming efficient in the use of the following word identification strategies for constructing meaning:**
  - **sounds-out to decode words**
  - **uses initial letters as a cue to decoding**
  - **uses knowledge of common letter patterns to decode words, e.g. th, tion, scious, ough**
  - **uses known parts of words to make sense of the whole word**
  - **uses blending to decode words, e.g. str-ing**
  - **uses word segmentation and syllabification to make sense of whole word.**

Attitude

The reader:

- is self-motivated to read for pleasure
- reads for a range of purposes
- responds sensitively to stories
- discusses favourite books
- may discover a particular genre, e.g. adventure stories (may seek out other titles of this type)
- shows a marked preference for a specific type of book or author
- makes comparisons with other texts read
- demonstrates confidence when reading different texts.

Teaching Notes

In this phase there is further development and refinement of reading skills and strategies. When reading appropriate text the reader reads fluently, recognising many words by sight and showing increased ability to integrate all three cuing systems. The reader has developed a range of strategies that provide options when confronted by unfamiliar words or phrases.

As students in this phase are consolidating their understanding of reading they need many opportunities to read independently to practise and further refine their reading strategies.

Discussion of concepts and vocabulary in reading conferences is important as readers in this phase may be able to decode words whose meaning they do not understand. The focus of need for adult support changes from negotiation of the print system to interpretation of meaning.

Help students to become critical readers by standing back from a text and thinking about its impact, implications and the view of the world that is being presented.

It is important for all students to engage in reading for different purposes using a wide range of reading materials.

Major Teaching Emphases

Making Meaning at Text Level
◆ **Create a climate which fosters critical thinking**
◆ **Help students to be aware of the view of the world presented by an author and how this affects different people**
◆ **Discuss with students the effect of texts on their own attitudes and perceptions**
◆ **Ensure that students read a range of texts for a variety of purposes**
◆ **Discuss the use of prior knowledge of:**
  – **the text topic**
  – **text structures**
  – **language appropriate for different text types**
◆ **Provide opportunities for :**
  – **making comparisons with other texts**
  – **identifying the main issues in a text and providing supporting detail**
  – **identifying cause and effect and predicting outcomes**
  – **identifying character traits from textual cues**
  – **analysing plots**
  – **interpreting symbolic or metaphorical meaning**
  – **discussing concepts and vocabulary**
  – **extracting and organising information**
• Ensure that charts, notices, lists, wall stories/poems/recounts/reports etc. are topical and in constant use as referents

- Provide opportunities for individual conferences when students can talk through their use of reading strategies, their perceived strengths and specific needs and other issues that are on their minds
- Read literature with students that extends their literary experience
- Use literature and informational texts to focus on aspects of language use and text structure
- Involve students in discussion and a range of activities before, during and after reading
- Provide opportunities for students to write every day, selecting text forms according to purpose and audience
- Focus on the use of print conventions during shared book sessions, proof-reading and editing activities
- Provide opportunities for retelling complex stories, including stories from shared reading sessions and independent reading

Making Meaning Using Context

◆ **Model and discuss:**
  - **prediction and confirmation strategies**
  - **use of syntactic and semantic cues**
  - **use of picture cues**
  - **use of context cues**
  - **re-reading**
  - **reading-on**
  - **substituting words**
- Model and discuss use of context cues to identify words:
  - sentence patterns
  - picture cues

Making Meaning at Word Level

◆ **Model and discuss word identification strategies:**
  - **use of graphophonic knowledge and 'sounding-out'**
  - **blending**
  - **letter and word patterns**
  - **sight words**
  - **using syllabification and segmentation**
  - **using knowledge of root words and word components**

At all phases:
◆ **foster children's enjoyment of reading, encouraging them to explore a variety of texts and take risks with confidence**
◆ **read to students every day and share your own enjoyment of reading**
◆ **encourage students to respond critically to texts they have read or viewed**
◆ **model reading behaviours and strategies for students to emulate**
◆ **encourage students to select their own books and read independently every day**
◆ **encourage students to share experiences related to reading and viewing**
◆ **talk to students about their reading and viewing**
◆ **provide opportunities for students to write every day for different purposes and audiences.**

◆ *Entries in bold are considered critical to the children's further development*

Behaviours to be Encouraged

Making Meaning at Text Level

- Using knowledge of the text topic
- Using language cues
- Using contextual knowledge
- Using knowledge of text structure
- Using knowledge of conventions of print
- On-going monitoring to ensure that reading is making sense
- Reflective and critical reading resulting in discussion and argument

Making Meaning Using Context

- Predicting and confirming strategies
- Re-reading
- Reading-on
- Having-a-go
- Using cues such as sentence patterns, picture cues, language appropriate to the text
- Sub-vocalising
- Using textual cues to identify words
  - sentence patterns
  - picture cues

Making Meaning at Word Level

- Using graphic and phonic knowledge
  - sounding out
  - blending
  - knowledge of letter and word patterns
- Using knowledge of sight words
- Using knowledge of syllabification
- Using knowledge of root words and word components such as prefixes and suffixes

Attitude:

- Having-a-go
- Reading for pleasure
- Responding to books sensitively and discusses them with others
- Showing preference for particular types of books

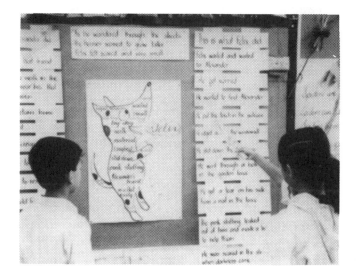

Teaching Strategies

Making Meaning at Text Level

- Plan activities where children are reading for different purposes:
  - Read recipes; children prepare the recipe as a class or as a group
  - Read menus; children select a particular meal and describe it to the class
  - Plan a game; children work together to plan a game. This requires the writing of specific directions for others to follow.
  - Use the newspaper for critical reading, finding and questioning information and looking for bias and stereotyping
  - Read cartoons, help groups to interpret a cartoon orally. Children then make up their own cartoons after analysing and discussing many examples of cartoons
  - Read riddles and puzzles; children can select puzzles they have enjoyed to read to the class. Puzzles can be used for revision of subject area material

- Continue shared book activities where children have the opportunity to be involved in:
  - identifying rhyme and rhythm and innovating on text
  - developing awareness of publishing techniques
  - developing knowledge of sound-symbol relationships
  - developing awareness of the inter-relationships of words
  - developing awareness of punctuation
  - enjoying and appreciating fairy-tale form
  - developing familiarity with titles, authors, illustrators and writing styles
  - confirming predictions
  - learning about genre
  - developing sight vocabulary
  - appreciating illustration and style
  - developing sense of style
  - making comparisons; *but make sure that the enjoyment of a story or the coherence of information is not lost by too much interruption to the reading.*

	Title Author	Title Author
Setting		
Characters		
Problem		
Resolution		
Timeline		

- Focus children's attention on literary aspects of the text, e.g. 'Did you notice things in the story/poem that made a pattern?', 'How long did it take for the story to happen?'
- Allow time for children to read independently every day. Plan 'DEAR' (Drop Everything and Read) sessions for appropriate times during the daily schedule. Emphasise the importance of reading quietly but allow children to share books if they wish. Ensure that there is a wide range of books or magazines for children to select from.
- Establish learning centres that will challenge and stimulate the children's interest. Develop centres around a theme, popular books or particular authors, e.g. Mem Fox, Roald Dahl.
- Set up a 'Language Exploration Centre' with problem-solving activities that encourage children to play with words, manipulate words, discover similarities, differences, relationships and origins.
- Plan to introduce children to a new author at least once a month by sharing select books with the class. Children could be encouraged to read other books by the author from the class collection.

- Ensure children are reading in all subject areas. Children need to become increasingly familiar with the specific language of each subject area.
  - Cloze activities can be used to associate meaning with particular words. Children should discuss their choice of words.
  - Newspaper articles are useful for developing a cloze passage. Select a passage which will be of interest to the children and delete every seventh word.

– Semantic maps help children to organise and extend information and concepts related to a particular topic.

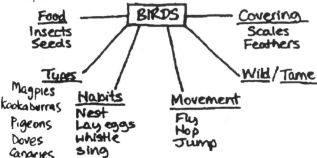

– Brainstorming and classification; children read and think about a topic. Brainstorm to find out all the facts they know about the topic. Categorise the information under particular headings. Children use this information to write a report.

– Read informational texts to children so they become aware of the layout and features of different text-types.

– Collect words related to a class topic. Children can discuss the meaning of their particular words.

– Use maps. Provide each child with a copy of a map of the local area. Use these as a basis for planning routes, e.g. the school bus route, the route children take to school, the postman's route.

– Organise walks around the community. Children can identify particular features shown on the map, e.g. shops, church, library, council buildings.

– Focus on the specialised symbols of maps. Plan activities that draw children's attention to abbreviations and symbols that indicate the places they are looking for.

– Use weather maps. Have children bring weather maps to school and discuss their patterns.

– Use timetables when planning excursions.

• Encourage children to take responsibility for the development of the class reading corner by contributing:
  – favourite books, magazines, comics
  – book reviews
  – story maps, dioramas
  – posters promoting books
  – projects
  – research paper.

BOOK REVIEW

TITLE OF BOOK: _____
AUTHOR: _____
CHARACTERS: Describe the main characters. How do they change throughout the story?
PLOT: What happened in the story? Which event do you think was most important?
SETTING: Where does the story take place?

• Provide opportunities for children to prepare board games relating to a particular story or novel. Children can work as a group to design the game incorporating characters, settings, main events from the story. This will involve the children in a lot of purposeful reading and writing.

• Work collaboratively with the class to develop a crossword puzzle based on a particular book.

• Make use of dramatic role play to further develop children's understanding of a text. After children have read a text the class is then divided into groups representing characters from the story. The reader acts as an interviewer reviewing the story by interviewing children about their feelings and responses to particular events.

• Help children to understand that reading is a way of enriching their lives:
  – Encourage children to relate events and characters from books to experiences and people in their own lives
  – Provide opportunities for children to prepare a talk or a display on a particular hobby or interest and recommend books on their topic
  – Read poems and stories about everyday experiences
  – Encourage children to keep a journal as a record of significant events in their lives and their feelings at different times
  – Read extracts from published diaries, e.g. *The Diary of Anne Frank*, *Penny Pollard's diary*.

• Model the story grammar of a traditional tale. Teacher and children work together to identify the main character, supporting characters, settings, sequence of events, complications and resolution. This information is represented in diagrammatical form. The strategy can be used effectively during and after reading or as a pre-writing activity to assist with planning.

• Foster children's awareness that a reader's contribution to a text is as critical as the writer's. Take one small passage or story and, after silent and reflective reading, encourage a range of children to offer their personal interpretations of the text. Value all responses and encourage further discussion. Make sure you do not accept one response as the 'right' answer.

- Continue to encourage children to stand back from a text and consider its impact on them as readers; encourage them to talk about how they deal with that impact.
- Involve the children in activities which focus on use of prior knowledge in reading. Children:
  - focus on story title and illustrations to make predictions. This can be small group or whole class activity.
  - work in small groups, listing their predictions and discussing focus questions such as, 'What do you think this story will be about? What kind of book do you think it will be?'
  - examine the table of contents and make predictions
  - relate the theme of the book to their own experiences
  - use their knowledge of story structure, e.g. 'It is a fairy tale so I know everyone will live happily ever after.'
  - use knowledge of author's style to make predictions about characters or plot
  - work with teacher to develop a semantic map related to the topic or theme of the book before reading, e.g.

```
                        ┌─── DOGS ───┐
   ┌──────┐  ┌──────────┐  ┌──────┐  ┌──────────┐  ┌───────┐
   │ care │  │ coverings│  │ food │  │  habits  │  │ types │
   └──────┘  └──────────┘  └──────┘  └──────────┘  └───────┘
   food       brown fur     meat       licks         corgi
   walks      black         bones      barks         collie
   brushing   spotted       dog biscuits  chases sticks
```

  - work with teacher to prepare 'What we know' and 'What we want to know' charts
  - discuss effective reading strategies.
- Involve the children in activities during reading. Children:
  - confirm or reject initial predictions made
  - discuss their initial predictions and then read aloud the section of the text that substantiates their predictions
  - make further predictions, i.e. predict how the story will end
  - read a paragraph and then plan questions to ask others in the group. Teacher asks a further question that will require children to make a prediction.
  - read part way through a story and then draw a cartoon or picture of how they think the story will end. Discuss pictures and then complete the story.
  - read to find the main idea of a paragraph
  - listen to or read a story from the stance of one of the characters and then talk about what this meant to them.
- Involve the children in activities after reading. Children:
  - confirm or reject initial predictions made
  - retell the story in small groups or with partners

- complete a semantic grid. Children are required to substantiate their responses from the text.
  Procedure:
  1 Children generate a list of character traits as a group
  2 Children make up the grid showing characters and their character traits
  3 Children discuss their choices

Characters	kind	evil	happy	sad	helpful	lazy
Red Riding Hood						
Grandmother						
Wolf						

- take part in cooperative cloze. Children interact on a cloze activity to suggest appropriate words to fill the gaps. Discussion is a very important part of this activity.
- take part in individual cloze practice. Children complete cloze activity individually and then get together to discuss choices. Prepare cloze by deleting every tenth, seventh or fifth word leaving the first and last sentence intact.
- take part in text sequencing. Cut the story into sections. The children are asked to arrange the story in its correct sequence and then justify their arrangements.
- construct a story map. Children develop a map that shows the sequence of events and identifies particular excerpts from the story. Children should have the opportunity to explain their map. The story map can also be used by a child when he/she is retelling the story.

- 'become' characters from a story and compare insights about the different reaction they experience
- write a follow-up adventure story using cartoons and captions
- select particular characters from the story and think what these characters might say after the story. Draw some speech bubbles and write in the conversation.
- select a character and draft a diary entry related to a particular event in the story

- discuss what they think has motivated and driven the author and talk about their own thoughts and reactions
- create a character acrostic by using the letters of a character's name to start words or phrases which describe the character
- complete a story summary focusing on: Who, What, Where, When

Who	What	When	Where
Little Red Riding Hood	Went to her Grandmother's place	Early one morning	On the other side of the woods

- sequence cartoon strips with the text removed, then write in their own speech bubbles.
- take on a character in the story and write a letter to another character
- write a report for the newspaper or a television program on an aspect of the story
- work in pairs as an interviewer and interviewee, a character from the story. One child prepares questions for the interview while the other child fills in an information sheet relating to his or her character.
- work in groups to develop a script from the text. This can be used for 'Readers Theatre' with children dramatising the story.
- complete a written retell of the story
- make comparisons with other books read

	The Three Billy Goats	The Three Little Pigs
Characters		
Setting		
Complications		
Resolutions		

- record descriptive phrases and group according to the aspect or character they describe
- compare:
  events and characters from books with a similar theme
  details presented by different authors writing on the same topics
  a particular location in a story with a location in another story
- develop crossword puzzles based on stories read
- write a poem about the story
- prepare a newspaper advertisement for the book
- write a television commercial advertising the book
- develop, 'Fact and Opinion' charts. Children record facts from the text and then add their own opinions on those facts.

- Help children develop appropriate strategies for reading for information.
- Developing skimming strategies.
  - Ask children to predict the contents of a book from its cover. Then have them skim the table of contents to confirm their predictions.
  - Children skim through reference books to check whether they are relevant to a particular topic
  - Encourage children to reflect on skimming strategies, identifying features of text that were helpful
  - Children skim through a section of the newspaper and then jot down their predictions about the content. They then read the article and compare their predictions with a partner.
  - Discuss strategies such as reading the first and last paragraph and the first sentence of each paragraph
  - Involve the children in skimming through a story after reading to prepare for retelling
- Developing scanning strategies. Encourage children to:
  - scan a telephone directory for a particular number
  - scan a television guide for specific information
  - scan reading texts for a specific information, e.g. the paragraph that shows how the character was feeling
  - scan to find a particular word in the dictionary. Have the children work in pairs to discuss the strategies they used to find the word.
- Involve the children in activities that develop the ability to extract the main issues or concepts.
  - Provide a caption for a cartoon or action illustration
  - Draw an appropriate illustration for a paragraph or story
  - Predict the plot of a story from the illustrations. Read the story to confirm or reject predictions.
  - State the essence of a paragraph. Ensure that children justify their particular choices.
  - State the essence of a chapter
  - Find the sentences that indicate the main issues and discuss choices
  - Look for supporting details to a specific main idea. This information can be categorised.
  - Skim a newspaper article to find the main points. Discuss the relationship between the headline and the significant ideas.
  - Select an appropriate title for a passage or selection
  - Select an appropriate title for a paragraph
  - Select an appropriate title for a poem
  - Re-read a story to gain the general idea to be portrayed in a retelling or a dramatisation
  - Find a sentence that contains the main idea of a paragraph. Sometimes the main idea is expressed in a number of sentences.
  - Make side headings for paragraphs in information material

- Discuss the relationship between the title and the plot of a story. Children may come to generalise that the author's title establishes a context for reading the particular story.

- Involve children in comparing information presented in texts. Compare:
  - characters or events from two different stories
  - style and illustrations
  - style settings
  - story events with aspects of their own lives
  - articles written on the same topic, e.g. information text on 'Spiders'
  - two books written by the same author
  - a narrative text about an animal with an information text about the same animal.

- Plan activities where children are involved in summarising and organising information. Children:
  - work in groups to summarise a piece of text. Summaries are then shared, and children are encouraged to ask clarifying questions. Children then tackle set questions as a group and draft their responses. They consider how best they could present what they have learnt about the text, e.g.
    written report
    oral report
    dramatic presentation
  - read a story and classify elements from the story under headings such as 'old and new', 'big and little', 'happy and sad'.
  - select their own headings under which information can be organised after reading a story
  - examine a bank of words and decide on categories into which they can be sorted

Characters	Setting	Feelings
Three Little Pigs Wolf Men with straw	brick house pot sticks	happy scared frightened

  - classify information in a story under the headings 'Could be true', 'Could not be true'. Children need to justify their conclusions.
  - analyse or organise information from a text into either a tree diagram or a retrieval chart
  - look for logical patterns or structures authors have used, e.g. comparison - contrast, cause - effect
  - summarise the text and make a 'miniature book'. The book is made up from small notebook sized pages. Appropriate illustrations accompany the text.
  - write diary entries for a particular character in a story
  - classify print materials in the classroom
  - recall a story sequencing events in an appropriate order

- sequence events that have been disorganised. This activity can be carried out using illustrations or jumbled paragraphs.
- predict events prior to and after a particular story
- change the sequence of a story to infer a different conclusion
- look at chapter headings or a table of contents to note the organisation of a book
- outline the contents of a passage or story for the purpose of relating information to others
- state relevant information about a book to help others decide whether they wish to read it, e.g. title, author, content, impressions, interesting quotes, where to get the book, other books by the same author.

- Provide opportunities for conferences where children discuss aspects of their reading. It is important to prepare children for reading conferences. Children need to have a clear understanding of the process and intentions of this type of interaction. Model appropriate questions and responses so children know what is expected of them. It is important to organise regular conferences with *all* children in the class. These may be organised on a small group basis or they may be individualised according to children's needs.

- Establish a clear purpose before each conference. It is worthwhile selecting a focus for conferences for the week, e.g. The focus may be:
  - a particular author
  - genre
  - story setting
  - story beginnings and conclusions
  - character descriptions.

- Use focus questions to help children prepare for a conference, e.g. Conference focus - 'a particular author':
  - How did the author describe the characters?
  - Where did the story take place?
  - What was the theme of the book?
  - How did the author keep you interested?
  - How would you describe the author's style of writing?
  - Does this author's style remind you of another author you know?

- Encourage children to evaluate their own reading. Teach children to:
  - articulate their difficulties
  - discuss the questions they ask about the text and any questions that weren't answered
  - discuss how they solved problems
  - become interested in their own strategies.

Examples of students' comments
- *I learned something about how I can read better ... I didn't realise that so many things happen in my head*

when I read … I realise that sometimes guessing wrong about what might happen in a book can help you enjoy a book better—as long as you do guess.
  – *If you don't understand something, you ask yourself why it is there. Some incidents don't seem to fit at first, but they do when you think about them. You don't understand until you read some more.*

- Provide the opportunity for children to keep reading logs where they can record any of the following:
  – a list of books read
  – comments on particular authors
  – responses to a particular text
  – book reviews
  – summaries of books
  – comments on personal reading strategies
  – plans for further reading.
- Encourage children to make use of the 'Who, What, Where, When' question framework when reflecting on a text.

Who	What	How	Where	When	Why
an old lady	travelled	horse	bush	early one morning	unhappy
a queen	lived	car	city		curious
a prince		walked	river		
a dragon			desert		
a koala				late one afternoon	

- Foster reflective and critical reading by modelling it yourself, e.g. 'In this book the airline pilot is a man and all the pictures show men flying and women as Flight Attendants. When I was on holiday, I saw men and women doing both jobs.'

  or

  'This book annoyed me because it seems to say that Jerry had no choice and couldn't have changed his mind about what he did. What do you think?'

  or

  'This advertisement makes me think I'll be beautiful if I use the cream. I don't think it will make much difference to my looks—but I expect it will make my skin smoother.'

  or

  'This story seems to take it for granted that people who have to leave their own country and come here will automatically think they are very lucky. How would you feel if you were a refugee and you read this story?'

Making Meaning Using Context

- Delete words that require children to use their semantic knowledge to predict, e.g. *'What a terrible storm, ' he said as — flashed and a loud — of thunder sounded outside.*
- Underline words that are difficult but have meanings explained in the text. Ask children to list these words and use the context to help explain the meaning of the words, e.g. *It was a strange* <u>coincidence</u>. *Both the twins were involved in an accident on exactly the same day.*
- Create a passage in which a non-word is used in place of a particular part of speech. Children can be encouraged to re-read the story providing different words that might make sense. Children can share and discuss their different versions, e.g. *Once upon a time a sapoon was preparing for a very important occasion. This sapoon had been asked to reveal his very special skills…*
- Use a Question Word Framework: Who? What? How? Where? When? Why? Children write a selection of words under each heading and then use the list to create stories. This helps children predict the type of words and the patterns of words found in connected discourse.
- Encourage children to use context and semantic cues when identifying words in content area texts. Have children brainstorm words they associate with topic or theme. Groups the words appropriately.

Use of Syntactic Cues

- Delete words which can be predicted by using knowledge of syntax. For example: *The boy was sitting in class gazing — the window. 'What did I just say?' — the teacher.* Children can use syntactic knowledge to predict the correct tense of the verb.

Making Meaning at Word Level
Use of Graphophonic Information
- Develop cloze activities in which graphophonic cues provide the information that enables children to choose possible alternatives, e.g. *The boys and girls were ex— because they were going on a school camp.*
- Work in groups to see how many different words they can construct from a grid, e.g.

n	f	p	b
r	ear	g	
w	ed	ing	cl

- Break words into syllables by listening to words and clapping the number of syllables they hear. Children can be given a blank grid, e.g.

in — form — a — tion

X	X	X	X

While the teacher reads the words, the children put a cross in a box for every syllable they hear.
- Identify words that rhyme and then ask the children to sort the words according to visual patterns.
- Fill in endings omitted form words in a story. Children compare their stories. They can be encouraged to prepare stories for each other.

'Word Solving Strategies', Judith Rivalland, Edith Cowan University

For Parents

How can I help my child with reading?

- Continue to read to your child if he/she enjoys it.
- Include humorous books when selecting books to read. Encourage your child to make up jokes or riddles, or humorous stories.
- Encourage your child to go to the local library regularly.
- Make sure you read some of the books your child enjoys so that you can share reactions and pleasure together.
- Ensure that your child knows what you value and enjoy reading yourself.
- Give your child book plates to stick inside his/her books.
- Encourage your child to draw and write about books and to write stories or factual information for others to read.
- Encourage your child to read to younger brothers and sisters.
- Read books that have been made into films or videos and encourage your child to talk about the differences between the books and the video or film.
- Ask your child what word would make sense when he/she becomes 'stuck' on a word. Encourage your child to have-a-go and read-on to get the overall meaning.
- Select a simple child's cookery book from the library and plan a cooking session. Encourage your child to read and follow the instructions.
- Encourage your child to find an interesting article/photograph from a newspaper and tell you about it. Suggest that it be taken to school and read/discussed with the class.
- Discuss favourite authors together and decide why you like them.
- If a child makes a mistake when reading aloud, don't interrupt the reading, allow time for self-correction. If the mistake doesn't alter the meaning, let it go.
- Draw the child's attention to weather patterns displayed in the paper and relate these to televised weather reports.
- Encourage your child to read and write letters, postcards, lists and messages. Accept spelling inventions. Provide attractive paper and unusual pens.
- Encourage your child to make birthday, Christmas and Easter party invitations. The child can write his/her own greetings and verses. You may even be able to make recycled paper together.

- Buy your child games that provide simple instructions to be read and followed. Play word games together.
- Encourage your child to enter competitions in the local newspapers or magazines.
- Encourage your child to make up, and perform, plays for the family, using own and other stories. Some children like to write simple scripts or draw up a plan for other children to follow.
- Continue to play numberplate games in the car. Relate numbers to letters of the alphabet, e.g. 372=cgb=Can't Go Back.
- Encourage your child to keep a diary or journal when on holiday. This is particularly valuable if you are travelling and the child is missing school.
- Involve your child in planning for holidays. Ask the child to list all the things to be taken. Obtain a map of the area and discuss the route you will be taking. Point out signs along the way.
- Encourage your child to help you find a particular street when you are using a street directory.
- Encourage your child to retell stories. Involve the family in swapping stories, e.g. 'I'll tell you a story if you tell me one.'

Independent Reading

In this phase readers competently integrate a range of strategies to make meaning. Reading is purposeful and automatic. Readers are only aware of the reading strategies being employed when encountering difficult text or reading for a specific purpose. Readers have greater ability to make connections between what they know and understand and what is new. They recognise obvious stereotypes in texts and may challenge texts, drawing on evidence from their own experience and knowledge.

Reading Interview - Marian

What is Reading?

'It's what you do for information on recreational purposes (enjoyment, pleasure). You can read to yourself, silently or out loud and you can read or listen to others read out loud.'
'Reading for information is used for project of assignments, to answer a question or just curiosity. Reading for enjoyment can also be from curiosity or perhaps pleasure, in case you're bored and many other reasons.'

How do you Read?

'Reading doesn't come naturally, although learning to read can be easier for some than others. You learn to read at school, at home, from teachers, parents, babysitters. Anyone else who knows how to read fairly well can teach you. You have to learn gradually, letters, words, sentences, paragraphs, pages, whole books! Some people can't read, this is known as illiterate. Right now you're reading what I have written. A lot of readers create images of what they're reading, every person's images are in some way different.'

Who Reads?

'People do, like you and me, because animals, birds and other creatures don't have the intelligence to. People who can't read can learn.'

What kinds of Books do you like to Read?

'I like to read any type of book really, though some topics appeal to me more than others. A few to mention are: adventure, comedy, romance, stories based on reality or something that's happened, etc. I like books, when they're creative, written well and the topic appeals to me.'

What do you do when you are reading and you don't understand something?

'When I don't understand what I'm reading I go through stages to help me find the meaning.
(a) Read the problem twice.
(b) Read the phrases before and after the problem.
(c) Refer to a dictionary or otherwise.
(d) Ask a reliable, trustworthy person who might understand.'

Independent Reading Indicators

Making Meaning at Whole Text Level

The reader:

◆ **can recognise and discuss the elements and purposes of different text structures, e.g. reports, procedures, biographies, narratives, advertisements, dramas, documentaries**

◆ **reads and comprehends text that is abstract and removed from personal experience**

◆ **makes inferences based on implicit information drawn from a text and can provide justification for these inferences**

◆ **returns purposefully to make connections between widely separated sections of a text**

◆ **makes critical comparisons between texts**

◆ **can discuss an alternative reading of a text and offer possible reasons why a text may be interpreted differently by different readers or viewers**

• talks with others about interesting or difficult content

• can justify own interpretation of a text

• comments and makes judgements on the ways authors represent people from different cultural and socio-economic groups

• is beginning to recognise and appreciate that authors manipulate language in a variety of ways to clarify and enhance meaning

• can recognise and discuss the elements and purposes of different text structures, e.g. biography, mystery

• reflects on and discusses issues and topics that have emerged when reading or viewing
  – challenges and criticises text and topics, offering supportive evidence
  – organises logical responses to a text
  – selects relevant information for own purpose
  – identifies and synthesises points of view
  – draws conclusions from text and generalises about information extracted from them

• may compare self and own experiences with fictional characters to enrich understanding

• reads and comments critically on materials such as news items, magazine articles, advertisements and letters in the press, identifying techniques and features designed to influence readers

• applies basic research skills effectively, e.g. identifies informational needs, uses knowledge of library organisation and text organisation and extracts relevant information from data base, catalogue or book.

Making Meaning Using Context

The reader:

◆ **uses a range of strategies automatically when constructing meaning from text**
  – **self-corrects**
  – **re-reads**
  – **reads-on**
  – **slows down**
  – **sub-vocalises.**

Making Meaning at Word Level

The reader:

◆ **uses word identification strategies appropriately and automatically when encountering an unknown word**
  – **knowledge of graphophonics**
  – **knowledge of word patterns**
  – **knowledge of word derivations, morphographs, prefixes, suffixes and syllabification.**

Attitude

The reader:

• may avidly pursue a favourite author. Books may be compared and recommended to others.

• feels strongly about reading preferences and can justify opinions

• is totally absorbed when reading

• sees books as a major source of information

• empathises strongly with admired characters in fiction.

Teaching Notes

In this phase readers have developed a personal reading style that emerges because of the range of different background experiences, interests, attitudes and skills readers bring to a text. Readers can make connections between what they know and understand and what is new. Readers can construct meaning and integrate a range of reading strategies when reading a variety of texts. Readers are usually only consciously aware of strategies being employed when reading for a specific purpose or when encountering difficult text. They are able to challenge and criticise texts, offering evidence which supports their arguments.

Readers in this phase need an individualised reading program that provides opportunities for reading across the curriculum and encourages the integration of strategies to improve their awareness and understanding of how to construct meaning from different texts. As readers become conscious of *how* they use reading strategies they gain more control over what they read and move towards higher levels of understanding and critical thinking.

Major Teaching Emphases

Making Meaning at Text Level

◆ **Teach students to:**
  - **articulate their reading difficulties**
  - **discuss the questions they asked of the text and any questions that weren't answered**
  - **discuss how they solved problems**
  - **select and use appropriate strategies when reading for different purposes**
◆ **Praise and encourage students when they show evidence of critical reading, listening and responding sensitively to their comments**
◆ **Teach students to identify and comment on different points of view in texts.**
◆ **Establish a language-rich environment presenting print in natural and meaningful contexts**
◆ **Provide opportunities for students to examine, analyse and discuss narrative and expository texts**
◆ **Teach students to:**
  - **analyse topics/questions**
  - **generate self-questions**
  - **select appropriate texts and compile reference lists**
  - **summarise and take notes**
  - **organise responses for reporting**
  - **compile bibliographies**
◆ **Develop the students' ability to read from a writer's viewpoint and to write from a reader's viewpoint**
• Establish individual reading programs
• Provide opportunities for individual conferences where students discuss aspects of their reading
• Present students with a wide range of reading materials

- Read to students every day from a variety of forms of text
- Make teaching purposes explicit to students so they understand the point of what they are being asked to do
- Model and discuss appropriate use of diagrams to help readers extract and organise important information
- Provide opportunities for students to play around with the genres of writing as a way of developing and reinforcing mastery and control of the genres and their conventions
- Teach students how to identify important information in texts
- Encourage students to reflect on and respond critically to texts
- Model and discuss how to support conclusions drawn from a text by citing evidence from the text and quoting external references
- Help students to become not only active readers and performers of text but also creators of their own texts
- Encourage students to re-write all kinds of texts for different audiences, e.g. re-write a chapter of an instructional textbook on science for readers younger than those for whom it was written
- Help students to become more conscious of the craft of writing and practise achieving the same kinds of effects in their own writing that they identify in other texts
- Encourage students to evaluate their own learning from the reading and writing activities developed in the reading program

Making Meaning Using Context

- Teach students how to monitor the effectiveness of reading strategies

Making Meaning at Word Level

- When reading difficult text encourage readers to be aware of any consciously integrated word identification strategies.

At all phases:

- ◆ **foster children's enjoyment of reading, encouraging them to explore a variety of texts and take risks with confidence**
- ◆ **read to students every day and share your own enjoyment of reading**
- ◆ **encourage students to respond critically to texts they have read or viewed**
- ◆ **model reading behaviours and strategies for students to emulate**
- ◆ **encourage students to select their own books and read independently every day**
- ◆ **encourage students to share experiences related to reading and viewing**
- ◆ **talk to students about their reading and viewing**
- ◆ **provide opportunities for students to write every day for different purposes and audiences.**

◆ *Entries in bold are considered critical to the children's further development*

Behaviours to be Encouraged

Making Meaning at Text Level

- Integrate knowledge of all language cuing systems
  - graphophonic
  - syntactic
  - semantic
  - pragmatic.
- Select and use relevant aspects of prior knowledge suitable for each text
  - personal experience
  - topic knowledge
  - text structure knowledge.
- Identify important information in text.
- Select and use appropriate strategies when reading for different purposes, i.e.
  - for pleasure
  - for information
  - to identify question and answer relationships
  - for research.
- Plan, monitor and reflect on strategies used in reading, i.e.
  - predicting
  - confirming
  - monitoring
  - sampling
  - self-correcting
  - summarising
  - evaluating.
- Critically respond to and reflect on text meanings and provide different levels of interpretations and points of view.
- Assess the effect of a text on student's own thinking
- Understand links between reading and writing. Rewrite chapters (or incidents or sections) of all kinds of books:
  - from different viewpoints
  - for different audiences
  - using the structures and styles of the original.
- Empathise or relate personal experiences to the behaviour of fictional characters.
- View incidents from the perspective of different fictional characters.
- Draw analogies from fiction to gain a heightened awareness of self and the world.
- Manipulate the genres of writing as a way of showing and reinforcing mastery and control of genres.

Making Meaning Using Context

- Select and integrate reading strategies, i.e.
  - syntactic strategies
  - semantic strategies
  - pragmatic strategies
  - read-on
  - re-read
  - slow down
  - use an outside source
  - substitute
  - sub-vocalise
  - use mental imagery
  - predict — substantiate
  - skim or scan
  - self-correct.

Making Meaning at Word Level

- graphophonic strategies
- syllabification
- knowledge of root words
- word derivation and word components
- review and reflect on efficiency of word identification strategies used

Attitude

- pursuing an interest or preference for a topic or text type
- swapping books and recommending them to friends
- discussing topics and arguing about issues that have emerged from texts.

Teaching Strategies

This material was written by Jack Thomson and adapted, with permission, for use by the First Steps Project.

Making Meaning at Text Level

- Organise a coherent wide-reading program in the class. The class reading program should involve a systematic procedure for helping students to find books that will speak to them most urgently. It should prompt them to read these books with greater interest and insight. Teachers need to ensure that activities do not become routine, hoop-jumping exercises that have little meaning to students. It is important to develop a comprehensive class library that includes novels by the same author, of the same period, similar topic or contrasting style.

- Have each student keep a reading journal or log as a written conversation with the teacher as well as with self. In the act of reading a text they jot down:
  - questions they ask of the text which they want, and expect to get, the answer to
  - predictions they make about what might happen
  - puzzles they are having with their reading
  - questions they want to ask in class about the text; that is, questions they don't know the answers to
  - points they want to make in class and which they want other student's opinions on.

  An example of 'interrogating the text'
  1. What is the significance of this particular detail/ event/form of words?
  2. How does it connect with other details/episodes..?
  3. What is this preparing us for? What kinds of things might (or could) happen?
  4. How does this event effect my interpretation of what has gone before?
  5. What am I learning about this character and his/her relationship with others? Why was he/she included in the story at all?
  6. Whose point of view is being presented? Why is the author offering this character's point of view here?

- Introduce a program of USSR (Uninterrupted Sustained Silent Reading) in which students (and teacher) read books of their own choice for fifteen minutes each day.

- Have students record their recommendations about library books read by writing on a slip of paper, pasted at the back of each book, their rating (from A to E or 'great' to 'boring') and/or descriptive comment, together with their signature.

- Organise plenty of small group work on texts read.

- Have students who have read the same book work in a group to prepare a performance on part of it, with the aim of persuading other members of the class to read the book, e.g.
  - a video or audio tape recording of a scene from a book with music and sound effects (re-writing prose fiction as drama)
  - a dramatic reading of an episode
  - a dramatisation of a poem
  - a display with maps, posters, dioramas.

  It is important to make sure that the active participation is followed by reflective evaluation.

- Encourage students to critically respond to and reflect on texts.

  There are many useful ways of giving book reports and responding to functional texts. Teachers should ensure that activities are meaningful and further enhance the students' understanding of the text. The following suggestions are meaningful alternatives.
  - Paint a mural of the story or a scene from the story
  - Make a book jacket with an inside summary
  - Write another ending for the story
  - Write a lost and found advertisement for a person or significant object in the story that you think would be a symbol of one of the characters. Tell why you chose this object and how it is a symbol of the story
  - Make a picture book of the most important parts of the novel
  - Make a dictionary of important terms used in the book
  - Make a poster to advertise the book
  - Make a timeline or show routes (and times) on a map
  - Make a tape-recorded report to the class—a radio broadcast review
  - Write a poem about the story
  - Give an illustrated oral report (postcards, drawings, etc.)
  - Write questions that you don't know the answers to and want to know the answers to, and discuss them in small groups
  - Think of new adventures or incidents you could add to the story
  - Write an unsigned letter from the point of view of a character, and have the rest of the class work out which character it is

– Write an imagined biography of one of the characters
– Write an account of what you might have done if you were in one of the character's predicaments
– Construct a stage and setting for a scene in the book
– Write a diary that might have been kept by a main character
– Organise a panel discussion of several people who have read the same story
– Organise interviews of people assigned to roles from the story
– Role-play the author, defending this book against critics on radio
– Give a sales pitch for the book to the class
– Prepare a plan to adapt the book for stage or on screen
– Write a letter to the author telling why you enjoyed the book
– Write about a true-to-life incident similar to one in the story
– Write as one of the characters many years after the incidents in the novel
– Write an imagined dialogue between characters in two books
– Write a newspaper report of an incident, as it might have appeared in a newspaper in the time and culture of the novel
– Select background music for scenes in the novel
– Compare characters faced with similar problems in different books
– Tell why you would like to meet a fictional character in real life
– Research fact from fiction in an historical novel
– Discuss the effect of setting on the behaviour and attitudes of the characters
– Play 'Who Am I?' with the class, using books members of the class are familiar with
– Create a greeting card that one character might send to another. Tell why it would be sent and the receiver's reaction.
– The main character is to receive an award at a ceremony. Design the award and tell why the person is to receive it.
– You are a millionaire suffering from a fatal illness. You are trying to decide what to do with your money. Tell which character you would leave your money to and why.
– Choose a scene from your book and rewrite it as if it took place two hundred years in the past or two hundred years in the future
– Choose a scene from your book and rewrite it as if it took place in one of these locations:
  on a desert island
  in Antarctica
  on an ocean liner
  in your town

– You are a newspaper reporter covering an event as you witnessed it
– You are a private detective assigned to follow the main character. Write a report on his or her activities over one period of time. Tell where she or he went, whom she or he saw, and what she or he did. Draw conclusions about the character's motives, values and lifestyle.
– You are a psychologist offering advice to the main character. Tell what the problem is and what advice you would give.
– You are a fortune-teller. Predict the future for the main character. Give details of where she or he will be and with whom, and what will happen. Link these predictions to events in the character's life as presented in the book.

• Provide opportunities for students to play around with the genres of writing as a way of showing and reinforcing mastery and control of the genres or conventions played with.
Students need to develop control of genres, not be dominated by them. Playing games with them, mixing them up deliberately, is a way of helping children achieve this mastery, e.g.
– Read Janet and Allan Ahlberg's *The Jolly Postman and Other People's Letters*. Discuss the way the authors have played around with conventions and literary knowledge. Get the students to do in their *own* writing of letters what the 'Ahlbergs' do.

Other stories students at this phase enjoy for the same reasons as outlined above are:
– Jan Mark's *William's Version* (In *Nothing to be Afraid Of*)
– Anthony Browne's *Bear Hunt*
– Shirley Hughes' *Chips and Jessie*
– the books of Raymond Briggs and John Burningham
– the poetry of Spike Milligan.

• Encourage students to rewrite all kinds of text for different audiences, e.g.
– rewrite a chapter of an instructional textbook on science for readers younger than it was written for
– rewrite a fable as a play script to be performed for a school assembly
– rewrite a short story as a radio play to be presented on audio tape
– develop a board game for younger students using characters and events from a novel
– rewrite a well known fairy story for older readers.

These learning experiences help students to develop knowledge of concepts rather than mimic forms of words.

• Develop the student's ability to read from a writer's viewpoint and to write from a reader's viewpoint, i.e.
– Encourage students to use the structures and styles of text they read, in their own writing.

– Develop their awareness of the craft of writing through discussion and questioning.
– Ask questions that focus attention on writing style, characters, use of conventions, literacy devices, setting, development of plot.

• Model and discuss appropriate use of diagrams to help readers extract and organise important information.

Illustrations, tables and diagrams are valuable aids to comprehension and learning. Teachers need to model the different diagrammatic forms so that children learn how to make such diagrams for themselves. Once children are experienced in using a number of diagrams, they can then decide which diagram to use in a particular situation.

Making Diagrams
Readers identify key information and interrelationships between ideas and transform them into graphic form.

Different types of Diagrams
1 Labelled Diagrams
2 Sequences of Pictures
3 Hierarchies
4 Flow Charts
5 Cycles
6 Structured Overviews
7 Modified Structured Overviews
8 Retrieval Charts
9 Venn diagrams
10 Tree diagrams

Labelling Diagrams
Children read a description and then draw and label a diagram presenting the main ideas.
– Discuss how diagrams can help with understanding and remembering text, e.g.
'A vacuum flask consists of two very thin walls of glass, a vacuum being between the two walls. Heat cannot be transferred by either conduction or convention through this vacuum. To prevent heat being transferred by radiation the interior of the glass is silvered.'

Sequencing pictures
A series of events in a story of a visit, steps in an experiment or instructions can be represented by a series of diagrams or illustrations.
– Children can use these pictures to retell the story or discuss an experiment or class visit, e.g.
Draw and label story map of *Cinderella*
Draw and label pictures showing the germination of wheat seeds.

Make a comic strip of the arrival of the First Fleet.

Creating Hierarchies
A hierarchy is a pyramid in which objects or people are ranked in order of importance. Usually there is only one object or person at the top, and an increasing number at each level below.
A hierarchy can be recorded as a simple diagram and does not require pictures.

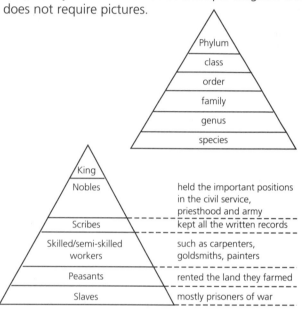

Making Flow Charts
Arrows are used to link important events and show their sequence. This helps to clarify and illustrate a chronological pattern most effectively, e.g.

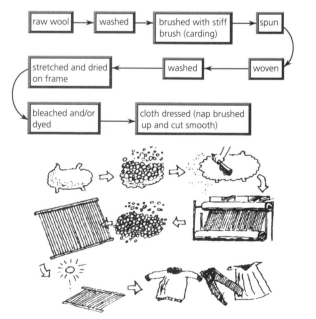

Identifying Cycles
A cycle is a series of events that occur over and over again in the same order. Cycle diagrams emphasise both the sequence of events and the fact that they recur in a never ending pattern, e.g.

Life History of the Frog

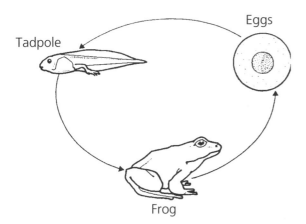

- Constructing Structured Overviews
  A Structured Overview shows the major concepts of a written passage and the relationships between them. It provides the reader with an overview of a topic prior to reading. It offers a framework for recording new information, ideas and details encountered while reading. A Structured Overview requires the reader to:
  – recognise and infer, if necessary, the major concepts;
  – distinguish between concepts and important details; and
  – recognise and infer relationships between concepts.
  The actual graphic organisation may be developed:
  – by the teacher and children during a lesson;
  – by children working in pairs or groups using a vocabulary list provided by the teacher; and
  – through a class brainstorming session beginning with a basic concept. This type of Structured Overview can be developed and modified as reading and knowledge of topic progresses, e.g.

Structured Overview for Landforms

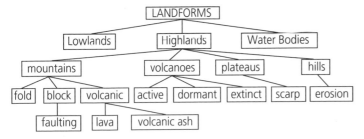

Note: Students should be encouraged to examine the relationships and present their own explanations.

- Modifying Structured Overviews
  After modelling the development of a Structured Overview teachers can ask students to fill in an incomplete model while they are reading. This makes them familiar with the format of an overview before they construct their own. The difficulty level can be controlled by varying the number of blank spaces to be filled.

- Making Retrieval Charts
  A Retrieval Chart organises information about a number of categories of objects or topics, so that they can be compared easily.
  Example:

	Football	Rugby	Soccer
No. of players			
Size/shape of ball			
Size/shape of field			
System of scoring			

The chart provides the reader with a graphic display that enables easy identification of details and comparison of qualities.

- Venn Diagrams
  Venn Diagrams represent sets and their relationships by circles or other figures (linking literary with mathematics and literacy with logical thinking).

- Tree Diagrams
  Tree Diagrams are very useful for helping students to organise and categorise their responses to a poem, e.g. they can identify the major themes, motifs, language characteristics, narrative voices, etc. and their connections with each other. Students find this a very productive tool in coming to make sense of a poem and in organising a coherent set of responses to it. *It is a tool of exploration, not a way of presenting a final report on that exploration.*

- Provide opportunities for students to examine and discuss sample texts so they are able to identify a range of different text structures in both narrative and expository forms.

It is important to provide opportunities for students to draw conclusions for themselves about genres of writing. If we want students to understand what the distinguishing features of a report, a narrative, a procedure are, we must ensure that they are exposed to and interact with many examples of each form.

Students can read different examples of a particular form and then make comparisons and identify defining characteristics. Teacher questioning is very important in drawing attention to the characteristics of the form. Students' comments can be blackboarded and used to draw up a set of rules for guidance when using this particular form.

Draw language activities from the content areas of the curriculum. Examine the different topics and decide how the content area can be used to develop the students' knowledge of particular text structures, e.g.

Social Studies	– diaries – historical fiction – myths and legends
Science	– reports – summaries – observation notes
Maths	– summaries – learning logs – nursery rhymes
Music	– ballad – sonnet – plays

Select a wide range of resources related to the topic ensuring that examples of different forms are included. Provide opportunities for students to use these resources independently.

Read examples of different forms related to a topic, e.g. a letter, a narrative, a description, and ask children to identify differences in structure related to the author's purpose.

Plan activities which will help students focus on particular aspects of a form, e.g.

– Change a narrative into a recount
– Change a procedure into a recount
– Write a poem about a story
– Rewrite a recount in the first person
– Rewrite a recount from one of the other character's points of view
– Rewrite texts and parts of fiction texts from different points of view from that (or those) point(s) of view presented in the text
– Compare a particular location in a story with either a location from another story or the students' present location
– Compare events or characters from two different stories on a similar theme or topic
– Encourage students to rewrite texts and parts of fiction texts from different points of view to that presented in the text. It is a way of getting students to take up opposition to the point of view of the author.

• Teach students how to identify important information in text.

Students need to be able to recognise those facts and details which are relevant and important because they support the main idea.

Activities that support the development of main ideas:

– sequencing scrambled sentences beginning with the sentence containing the main idea.
– skimming a newspaper article to find the main idea. Discuss the relationship between the headline and the main idea
– selecting an appropriate title for a paragraph
– identifying key words and phrases in a text. This should be done initially as a whole class activity then later in small groups or pairs. The emphasis is on justifying the choice of key words:

Students need to become aware that effective key words:

– must be specific enough to be meaningful in isolation
– will target the memory and allow for recall of specific supporting detail.

Begin with a single sentence related to the current topic and ask children to pick out or underline the key words or phrases. Sentences should gradually be made longer and more complex.

Change one key word in a sentence or question and discuss the difference this makes to the meaning.

Involve students in small group discussion after reading a selected paragraph. Students discuss the main idea of the paragraph. Differences in interpretation should be discussed. Identify particular words or phrases that might lead to differing understandings.

When students have read an important paragraph, i.e. one with an important main idea, have them choose from a multiple-choice list the phrase that best states the main idea. At the same time students must state why the other choices are inappropriate. Provide them with the following list as a guide in the decision making.

Statement may be:

– irrelevant
– too specific
– too general
– main idea, because it is the right level of generality.

Ask students to identify irrelevant sentences that have been inserted into paragraphs. Select text related to a current class topic or from a book the students are familiar with. Use a visual model to explain how a main idea relates to the details that support it.

For example:

A sun in which the rays are the details

A boxed outline which emphasizes the fact that details are logically subordinate to main ideas

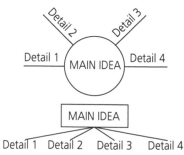

Written by Jack Thomson for the First Steps Project

Making Meaning Using Context

- Teach awareness, monitoring and adjusting strategies to help students make meaning or to recognise and adjust when the meaning is unclear. These strategies are used interactively and continuously.

Awareness strategies
Talk about:
- topic or background knowledge which may help comprehension
- level of comprehension required
- purpose for reading
- different reading styles for different purposes
- text organisation
- text inaccuracies
- differences in explicit and implicit information.

Monitoring strategies
Include:
- checking understanding by:
  - summarising information
  - paraphrasing information
  - synthesising information
- Integrating prior knowledge with new text information
- evaluating information
  - confirming predictions and hypothesis
  - evaluating consistency of main ideas and details.

Adjusting strategies
Include:
- re-reading
- backward-forward searching
- self-questioning
- locating point of mis-comprehension
- sustaining information from the text.

- Encourage students to predict what will happen and then to confirm their predictions as they read.
- Model strategies and allow students to practise them in context.
- Ensure that students have a reasonable sight vocabulary of words commonly seen in books, these are best taught in context.

Bruce Shortland-Jones

Making Meaning at Word Level

- Continue to explore word meanings, derivations and roots.
- Discuss the ways in which word meaning has changed over time.
- Encourage readers to read an extremely difficult segment of text, stopping to analyse specific word attack strategies as they are used.

For Parents

How can I help my child with reading?

- Recognise and be proud of your child's successes in reading.
- Ensure your child is exposed to a wide range of reading materials, i.e. newspapers, letters, recipes, TV guides, magazines, puzzle books.
- Provide a quiet, well-lit study area.
- Make sure your child uses the library regularly and encourage him/her to take younger children along.
- Encourage your child to read for different purposes, i.e.
  - reading biographies and novels
  - reading and explaining instructions for using new appliances
  - reading interesting articles from the community newspaper
  - reading to younger brother and sister
  - reading to find out more information about a topic.
- Take an interest in books written by favourite authors. Talk about them. Give them for presents.
- Encourage your child to talk about books he or she has enjoyed or disliked. Foster thoughtful criticism and comment.
- Support the learning process by guiding and advising. This doesn't mean doing the work for your child. Talking things through is very important.
- Talk to your child's teacher about homework expectations. Ask if there is anything further you can do to help.
- Let your child see that you sometimes need to discuss and clarify issues to help your understanding.

- Support your child's school research tasks by:
  - taking your child to the local library to find appropriate books
  - encouraging your child to jot down key issues about a topic
  - helping your child to classify this information
  - encouraging your child to explore the topic further by brainstorming topic-related questions using a 'Question Word' framework—'Who', 'How', 'When', 'If', 'Where', 'What', 'Why'.
  - encouraging your child to use the following procedures when taking notes, e.g.
    Short Notes
    key words and phrases with the
    reference book open
    Long Notes
    own sentences with
    the reference book closed.
- continue to discuss ideas, statements and underlying beliefs which are evident in newspapers, books and television programs.

PHASE 6

Advanced Reading

In this phase readers are confident and efficient in their control and use of appropriate reading strategies. They can critically reflect on and respond to text, by providing different levels of interpretation and points of view. They can deconstruct texts and make explicit their underpinning ideologies.

A Range of Comments from Readers

Good books are different. They are unpredictable. They look at unusual topics or ordinary things in unusual ways. They help you to think about things you take for granted, by letting you see ordinary things in ways you haven't thought about before.

On involvement and detachment in reading literature
Sitting back reading, you don't have the same feelings as the character himself has because you are not in his position but judging. It's like looking at a soccer match from the stand where you can see the mistakes and the tactics that go wrong, but the person playing is doing his best under pressure and can't see the patterns, you can. Some kids like to be backseat drivers in reading but they might think the novel is life when its only a picture of life. It's not actually happening. It shows you what the writer thinks life is like, what sorts of things are likely to happen and you're trying to learn what his view of life is like.

What active reading means
The characters in a novel are inside my head. Everything that takes place in the book takes place inside my mind. I produce the meanings in my head like the director of a play.

Constructing mental images in reading
While I'm reading I have a continuous movie in my head, only it's slower than a real movie. When I stop reading and start again later I read again the last page I've read to pick up my picture again. But my movie is not one of clear pictures like on film. When it comes to details on the face you don't see too much. It's more a feeling about a person.

Identifying important elements of novels
At the beginning I like to think what's going to happen towards the end, what changes might take place, and what things are going to be the same. You want to know if the characters will solve their problems, if they will continue to make the same mistakes or if they will learn from them, and what this all shows about them as people. At the end I like to compare events with the beginning and think about what's changed and why.

The value and appeal of fiction
Reading literature helps you to learn about life. The books take you far beyond what you have experienced yourself, so you understand something about the way people behave in the sorts of situations that haven't happened to you, but might happen sometime.
I like books which have suspense, that even after the first paragraph intrigue you so much that you must read on and find out what happens in the book.

Advanced Reading Indicators

Making Meaning

The reader:

◆ critically reflects on and responds to text, providing different levels of interpretation and adopting alternative view-points

◆ can stand back and reflect on own reactions to authors' perceived ideologies and positions

◆ recognises specific language forms such as figurative language, jargon and technical language

◆ recognises and describes the purpose and structure of different genres

◆ reflects personal interpretation of a text through oral reading

◆ recognises and responds to text complexity, e.g. ambiguity and conflicting messages in text

◆ can compare and contrast different points of view

◆ can identify and integrate layers of facts and concepts within a text

◆ can identify and discuss different authors' styles

◆ can recognise texts as 'cultural constructs' and can analyse the cultural beliefs underpinning texts

◆ can synthesise information within and across texts

◆ is able to select, use, monitor and reflect on appropriate strategies for different reading purposes

◆ is able to interrogate texts, articulating problems and formulating relevant questions

◆ can select key information and ignore irrelevant material

◆ can apply understanding of text structure to the acquisition, organisation and application of information

◆ can formulate and apply research strategies

◆ can recognise and analyse bias, propaganda and stereotyping in texts

◆ can draw on literary and cultural repertoires to construct meanings in order to compare the perceived world view of an author with own.

Attitude:

The reader:

• uses reading to enter worlds beyond personal experience

• confidently handles new texts

• responds sensitively and perceptively to literature

• reads literature with emotional involvement and reflective detachment.

Teaching Notes

In this phase readers are confident and efficient in their control and use of appropriate reading strategies. They can monitor, evaluate and describe their ability to construct meaning in a range of different texts. They can critically reflect on and respond to text by providing different levels of interpretation and points of view. Readers are able to deconstruct texts and make explicit *their* beliefs and ideas as well as those of the author. They appreciate that a text will be read differently by people from other socio-cultural backgrounds.

Major Teaching Emphases

◆ **Develop and monitor individualised reading programs, with the purposes and guidelines made explicit to, and negotiated with, students**
◆ **Encourage readers to monitor and evaluate the effectiveness of personal reading strategies**
◆ **Model and discuss appropriate ways to help readers extract and organise important information**
◆ **Provide opportunities for readers to respond critically to and reflect on text, i.e.**
  – **synthesise information in text**
  – **critically recognise and analyse bias and propaganda**
  – **compare and contrast different points of view**
◆ **Model and discuss the supporting of personal conclusions from within text and by using outside references**
◆ **Emphasise writing through reading. Integrate reading and writing programs. Help students to read from a writer's viewpoint and write from a reader's viewpoint**
◆ **Provide opportunities for readers to analyse and compare the structure of texts**
◆ **Provide opportunities for readers to analyse author 'styles' and writing craft**
◆ **Study literary criticism, theories and models**
◆ **Help students to understand that readers interpret texts in different ways and that one text can have many meanings**
• Provide access to a wide range of reading materials, including more complex text structures
• Encourage readers to discuss their ability to construct meaning in different texts
• Continue development of research skills over a range of narrative and expository texts
• Involve students actively in performance and presentation of texts and then provide opportunities for them to evaluate reflectively what they have learnt from these activities
• Involve students in planning activities for their own group work on text; that is, students can occasionally/often be asked to:
  – work out the issues to be explored in a text
  – devise the assignments for the work—both written assignments and performative/ presentational activities
• Encourage students to keep a reading journal and provide clear guidelines and specifications for the activities to be carried out

At all phases:

◆ **foster children's enjoyment of reading, encouraging them to explore a variety of texts and take risks with confidence**
◆ **read to students every day and share your own enjoyment of reading**
◆ **encourage students to respond critically to texts**
◆ **model reading behaviours and strategies for students to emulate**
◆ **encourage students to select their own books and read independently every day**
◆ **encourage students to share experiences related to reading**
◆ **talk to students about their reading**
◆ **provide opportunities for students to write every day for different purposes and audiences.**

◆ *Entries in bold are considered critical to the children's further development*

Behaviours to be Encouraged

- Controlling and integrating knowledge of all language cuing systems
  - graphophonic
  - syntactic
  - semantic
  - pragmatic
- Selecting and using relevant aspects of prior knowledge suitable for each text
  - personal experience
  - topic knowledge
  - text structure knowledge
  - socio-cultural knowledge
  - ideological understanding
- identifying important information in text
- Recognising and critically analysing bias and propaganda
- Selecting and using appropriate strategies for different purposes of reading, i.e.
  - pleasure and relaxation
  - gaining information
  - aesthetic appreciation, e.g. poetry
  - research
- Planning, monitoring and reflecting on strategies used in reading, i.e.
  - predicting
  - confirming
  - monitoring
  - sampling
  - self-correcting
  - summarising
  - forming mental images
  - filling in gaps
  - drawing on repertoire of personal experience, cultural knowledge, values and beliefs
  - making sympathies explicit
  - matching values with author
  - deconstructing
- Critically responding to, and reflecting on, text meanings and providing different levels of interpretation and points of view

Teaching Strategies

Written by Jack Thomson for the First Steps Project

- Organise a substantial wide-reading program, with the purposes and guidelines made perfectly explicit to, and negotiated with, students. A teacher in the Bathurst research program explains one way of linking the wide-reading program with the close-reading work on a shared class text:

  'With each novel studied, I like to provide an additional class library of novels by the same author, of the same period, similar topic, similar or contrasting style. Often given an insight into one novel, students are eager to try another in the same vein. This develops a greater awareness of style.'

- Help students to become increasingly conscious of their productive reading strategies, by slowing down their reading processes. One of the ways this can be done is to teach a poem or short story (or factual expository/report) by revealing its text line-by-line or sentence-by-sentence. A variation of this is to read the opening paragraph of a short story or novel (or informational text) and ask students to discuss their expectations, mental images, gap-filling activities and so on.

- Help students to explore, analyse and articulate their own reactions/responses to literature they have read, beyond such vague generalisations as 'boring' or 'great' by, for example, providing them with copies of conflicting reviews of a book and asking them to mark with a tick the passages of each review which they agree with, and a cross those passages they disagree with. In looking over what they have ticked and crossed such students become much clearer about their own judgment of the book and are thus better prepared to express and reflectively explore their own interpretations and the repertoires they have brought to such books to make them construct the interpretations as they have.

- Encourage students to keep a reading journal and provide clear guidelines and specifications for the activities to be carried out.

- Discuss journal entries with students.

- Invite students to read back over their journal entries periodically and make explicit what they have learnt about texts, about their own reading processes, about their own repertoires of experience, cultural knowledge and beliefs, and about their own cultural construction.

- Model, discuss and get students to use a range of note-making procedures, so that note-making really becomes a medium for personal discovery and reflection, and an aid to the development and articulation of response and meaning construction.
  (i) Making column notes is helpful as preparation for class discussion and for moving into continuous prose of a more sustained, coherent and analytical kind. The aim is always to help students to become more aware of the significance of what they read and to be able to make interpretative generalisations about them.
    - Students keep two running commentaries as they read a novel, with the left-hand page used for recording what happens and the right-hand page used for commentary, speculation and making connections with personal experience.
    - Students keep a chapter chart before their reading of a text. The columns for the note-making are headed Chapter, Number, When, Where, Who, What, Events, and Why. These columns are filled in as briefly as possible from a source of reference when finding specific incidents later to illustrate points in essays and discussion. For novels with a complex time sequence this kind of chart can make students conscious of aspects of structure.
    - Students can become more perceptive about characterisation and listing or summarising each main character's actions in one column, indicating the interpreted motives and predicted consequences of them in a second and third column, and drawing conclusions about the character's role and significance in a fourth column.
    - Students can be helped to visualise stage action in drama texts and reflect on its progressive significance by summarising the stage movements and events in narrative form in the left-hand column and commenting on the reasons for the stage directions in the right-hand column. Making diagrams helps students to begin systematising their fragmentary responses into coherence.
    - Representing the structural patterns of novels, for example, when the narrative order and the chronological order of events are different.
    - Showing the thematic relationships and shared motifs of different poems by one author, or different newspaper articles on the same topic.
- Thematic work
  - the multiple sources approach: using related film, photograph, song, verse and prose extracts from

fiction, non-fiction, newspapers, magazines, television, records. Beginning with personal experience and/or reading, students move into talking, dramatic improvisation, writing, cooperative presentations and wider related reading

- the multiple text approach: using a number of texts linked by a shared theme. This involves, for example, comparing the different responses and attitudes of writers to similar topics and/or the different methods they use to communicate similar themes. Sometimes, five or six different groups in a class might be given different texts (novels, articles, history books) on the same general topic, for example, war, and then report back to the rest of the class in a plenary session where comparisons and contrasts are drawn
- genre studies: science fiction, the sonnet, the mathematics textbook, for example
- author studies

• Group performance activities
  - prepared readings/dramatisations, live and on radio and video with sound effects and musical backing
  - role playing the author of a book or a character in fiction and being interviewed as in a press conference
  - mock trials of appropriate characters in books
  - debating issues raised by a book
  - rewriting and presenting in another medium; for example, scripting a short story as a radio play, and then presenting it on audio tape
  - making board games from novels structured as quests or escapes; for example Tolkien's *The Hobbit*
  - conducting newspaper, magazine, radio and television advertising campaigns for a book to present to fellow students

• Involve students in writing activities requiring *imaginative recreation* of texts. Students can explore and interpret texts by recreating all or parts of them in different forms or media, through different viewpoints or narrative modes, in modernised versions, and/or in the same form as the original but presenting an oppositional ideology. This requires them to master aspects of the rhetoric and style of the original texts and thus develop greater consciousness and control of fictional constructedness, e.g.
  - writing newspaper or magazines reports of events in novels
  - writing stories, poems, drama sketches from newspaper or magazine reports
  - rewriting third person character exposition as interior monologue or the reverse
  - writing contemporary Aboriginal legends
  - writing texts (e.g. 'The Lord's Prayer') in different idioms: ocker, hippie, etc.

• Teach students methods of deconstructing texts. Deconstructing literature, media texts, and all artefacts

of cultural production is aimed at developing an understanding of the ways in which the language of any text works to produce its meanings and to communicate its ideology. In deconstructing texts students will come to:
- understand the way ideologies are communicated
- understand the processes of their own cultural shaping
- learn how to use the rhetorics of texts for their own purposes.

• Activities could include:
  - examining the language of character construction (the adverbs and adjectives used to describe characters, etc.) the language that creates the reader's sympathy and antipathy, the narrative viewpoint and the values being promoted or denigrated by it
  - comparing the openings of different novels/poems/ history texts, etc., by the same author to discover any general stylistic characteristics
  - identifying the language of different authors to communicate mood, emotion, atmosphere in specific passages, and going on to:
      rewrite some of the passages, changing the mood or emotion to its opposite (e.g. from impending disaster to expected happiness)
      rewrite one authors' description in the style of another author
      use the same stylistic methods to communicate similar feelings about personal experiences in the lives of the students themselves
  - exploring and comparing the narrative methods of different texts and experimenting with such narrative viewpoints in writing from personal experience (e.g. writing about the same event from a number of different viewpoints)
  - presenting to students the lines of a poem or the paragraphs of a short story (or instructional text) and asking them, at each stage, to explain how they think the text will develop, and how each new line or paragraph confirms, modifies or alters their previous expectations and interpretations
  - showing students several drafts of professional writers' work and discussing the effects of, and possible motives for, specific revisions
  - mixing into a text a section from another text and asking them to identify the part that doesn't fit and to explain their decision
  - playing around with the structures of different discourses; for example, a formula for writing a novel, such as C + P + T + I + X = NOVEL (where C is character, P is place, T is time, I is incident and X is climax) by offering a range of alternatives for each item, such as: the character can be villain, coward, fool, cheat, etc. and child, old man, heiress,

journalist, etc.; place can be city street, political meeting, restaurant, etc.; and so on
  – transporting the elements of a text: rewrite sections of a novel, for example, changing the sex, class, race, nationality, and age of the characters to make transparent the biases of the author (for example change the male hero into a female, the working class thief into a wealthy businessman, the foolish Russian into an Englishman, the Vietnamese waiter into an Australian and so on). Textual silences and contradictions become pretty clear to students in this kind of work.

- In activities like these, the important thing the teacher is emphasising is not that students understand the meanings and methods of a particular book, but that they can read any text, have insight into how it works and how its meanings are produced, and also have a model for their own experimental writing. Formal analysis of this kind is a means to an end of helping students to understand how social values are constructed and communicated in language so they can interpret the ideological assumptions and implications of all that they read.

- Provide opportunities for students to *write imitations and parodies* of works by famous and published writers. In this way students learn to use the rhetorics of established writers, as well as to read the ideologies of texts. Students can bring imitations of poems, for example, by published poets, and offer three versions of the same poem, one written by the famous writer and two imitations written by them, and invite their peers to say which is the original 'famous' version. If it is difficult for others to know which is Lawrence Ferlinghetti's poem and which is Bobby Thornton's in 10D, then the romantic notion of a supremely gifted creative talent, or a divinely inspired artefact we are bidden to revere becomes nonsense. If students can write like a media personality or like a supremely gifted, divinely inspired, author, then they are in the same league as such luminaries. The binary opposition between writers and readers is broken, and students are using the rhetorics of the masters to become makers of their culture, not just receivers and potential victims of it. They have textual power.

- Encourage students to *tell and write texts of their own*. For example, getting students to tell their own stories and anecdotes in their own voice. Personal experience of school, home, peer group and society, together with the more fictitious tall stories and yarns they tell one another leads logically into the writing of more sustained stories. After all, written anecdotes differ from true experiences told orally in two ways: they are embellished, and they are more consciously shaped in a literary way to meet the demands of an audience not immediately present. Short stories represent the outcome of the same process of conscious literary

shaping but taken much further. Not only is there embellishment, modification, addition and deletion of events and details, but also there is the need to move from an egocentric viewpoint to experimentation with a range of narrative perspectives; to stand back from one's own personal feelings and make conscious decisions about the ordering of events (structure) and about such matters as tone and style. The stages of progression from spoken anecdote to written fictional story could be something like the following, although this sequence is not offered as an inflexible routine:
  (i) sharing personal experiences, yarns, tall stories in small groups
  (ii) taping monologues, after the details have been rehearsed and worked out in the more informal small group situation
  (iii) writing versions of the spoken stories
  (iv) writing fictional short stories, with all the additional shaping, invention and literary construction that this process requires
  (v) analysing and comparing the (quite different) language characteristics of the finished literary story and the first written version of the spoken story.
In this activity plenty of opportunities should be provided for individual conferences where students discuss aspects of their writing with trusted peers and with the teacher.

For Parents

How we can help each other with reading?

- Look for opportunities to discuss and share excerpts and ideas from a variety of different reading materials.
- Value your own reading and be informed by that of your child. Widen each other's horizons.
- Discuss ways in which tasks can be handled. Recall strategies that have been effective in the past.
- Recognise that both you and your child may have quite different ideas about what you want to read and respect choices made. Broaden reading experiences by exchanging books.
- Provide a quiet, well-lit study area.

Part IV

Profiles of Reading Development

To make recording easier for teachers, student profile sheets, that can be photocopied, are included in this book. They enable teachers to record the progress of individual students, and to compile a class profile.

The following records are included:
- student profile sheets for self-assessment
- whole class profile sheets using all the indicators
- whole class profile sheets using key indicators only.

Note:
An individual student profile sheet that will record progress throughout the primary years is included as a fold-out at the beginning of this book.

Student's Profile Sheets

The student's profile sheets for each phase provide lists of skills, understandings, strategies and attitudes that both the student and teacher can look for when assessing reading development.

Why use Student's Profile Sheets?

Students and teachers can work together to set and monitor goals in reading, using the profile sheets. Students could also be encouraged to show their parents when entries are made on the sheet.

How to use the Student's Profile Sheets

The profile sheets can be kept in student's personal files and updated from time to time, perhaps in student/ teacher conferences. Young students may need help to use the sheets but older students can be encouraged to take responsibility for their own reading development.

When would you use the Student's Profile Sheets?

The student's profile sheets can be used at regular intervals or incidentally during individual conferences.

PHASE 1: Role Play Reading

Name: _____ Date: _____

Look what I can do	not yet	some-times	always
• Hold the book the right way up.			
• Turn the pages by myself.			
• Talk about the pictures.			
• Point to the words.			
• Read my name.			
• Point to the first letter of my name in other words.			
• Know the meaning of some signs I see in the streets, shops and classroom.			
• Choose a favourite book.			
• Talk about and tell favourite stories.			
• Join in with songs and rhymes.			
• Know when someone has left out a bit of a favourite story. Know which page a favourite bit comes from.			
• Tell stories to myself or teddy, saying things like 'once upon a time' or 'happily ever after'.			
• Look at a book and tell a story to myself, using the pictures to help me.			
• Talk about people, animals or things in books which are like family, pets or things I know.			
I like: • Having stories read to me.			
• Telling stories to myself, other people or pets.			
• 'Reading' books.			
• Joining in telling the stories as they are read to me.			
• Hearing stories again and again.			

PHASE 2: Experimental Reading

Name: _____ Date: _____

Look What I can do	not yet	some-times	always
• Point to some words and say what they mean.			
• Understand that a story in a book is always told in the same words.			
• Point to some letters, especially those in my name.			
• Tell people what some signs and notices say.			
• Use words like book, chapter, word, letter, number.			
• Understand that I have to speak slowly if someone is writing down what I say.			
• Tell people what a story is about.			
• Retell a story and remember to say who it is about and what happened.			
• Say or sing most of the alphabet.			
• Tell the sound that some letters stand for.			
• Point to words as they are read (when I want to!)			
• Talk about how the people and animals in books are like or not like the people and animals I know.			
• Find a word which fits a gap in a story.			
• Sometimes I know what a word is by looking at the first letter.			
• Ask if I don't understand something.			
• Make good guesses.			
I like: • Reading.			
• Listening to stories.			
• Joining in and acting out stories.			
• Choosing books.			

PHASE 3: Early Reading

Name: _____ Date: _____

Look what I can do	not yet	some-times	always
• Read some words in books and find the same words in other places too.			
• Think of sensible words to fill gaps in a story.			
• Read the stories or sentences that I have written or dictated.			
• Tell what a story was about after it has been read and remember special bits about the people and what they did.			
• Sound out words that I don't know.			
• Go back and read a bit again if I forget what it's about.			
• Use pictures to help me read.			
• Guess what a word might be about.			
• Guess what a word might be if I'm not sure.			
• Point to words as I read them if I am reading something hard.			
• Use words I can see around me or words I know I have read before to help me learn.			
• Tell if words sound the same, like 'zoo' and 'you'; or look the same like 'door' and 'floor' and 'hood'.			
I like: • Having-a-go at reading new words.			
• Listening to stories.			
• Talking about stories.			
• Choosing books.			
• Reading for fun.			
• Reading to find things out.			

PHASE 4: Transitional Reading

Name:_____ Date:_____

Look what I can do	not yet	some-times	always
• Think of things I already know about a topic when I'm reading a book.			
• Tell other people what a book was about, whether it was a story or a book of information.			
• Give people more detailed information about a book if they ask for it.			
• Tell people what I think about a book and whether I agree or disagree with what it says.			
• Tell people why I think the way I do about a book.			
• Guess what is going to happen in a book and say why.			
• Tell when I've made a mistake and put it right.			
• Have-a-go at reading words I don't know.			
• Talk about how a story or an information book is put together.			
• Sound words out.			
• Read some words which I can't sound out, because I know how the letters go together (like: the, sh, …tion, …ough, …ight).			
• Break a word down into syllables.			
• Guess a word because I know another one like it, e.g. circle, circuit, circumference, or sign, signal, signature.			
• Understand why capital letters, full stops, commas, exclamation marks and speech marks are used.			
• Use my voice to show the meaning when I read aloud.			
• Tell when an author is trying to make me think about something his or her way.			

continued on next page

PHASE 4: Transitional Reading (continued)

Name: _____ Date: _____

Look what I can do	not yet	some-times	always
I like: • Reading for my own pleasure.			
• Reading to find things out.			
• Having-a-go at books which are interesting but a bit hard.			
• Talking about books and the way they make me feel.			
• Particular books and authors.			
• Comparing one book with another.			
• Thinking about whether a book is like real life or whether it's just the way the author sees it.			

PHASE 5: Independent Reading

Name: _____ Date: _____

Look what I can do	not yet	some-times	always
• Feel as if I've experienced things when I've really only read about them.			
• Work out a new idea or piece of information from a book.			
• Understand that different people will read things differently and try to see their points of view.			
• Tell when an author is trying to brainwash me.			
• Find the main idea and key information in a book.			
• Point to ways authors have used language to show that something is important, funny or sad, etc.			
• Describe how different texts are written in different ways, e.g. a report, a mystery story.			
• Make a good guess about the meaning of an unknown word by making sense of what is being said.			
• Use my imagination to create more meaning for myself.			
• Use my knowledge about how different texts are constructed to help me understand them, e.g. by looking at the opening sentence, the section headings and the conclusion.			
• Predict what might happen next.			
• Suggest why things might happen.			
• Summarise a text.			
• Draw conclusions.			
• Make inferences.			
• Describe how the purpose of a book dictates the way it is written.			
• Use my knowledge of the subject, the context, the sounds letters represent, word derivations, and the way a sentence is written, to help me.			

continued on next page

PHASE **5:** Independent Reading (continued)

Name: _____ Date: _____

Look what I can do	not yet	some-times	always
• Understand that I read different texts in different ways. For instance, I read a difficult text slowly and may point to the words; I skim a text to find key words.			
• Read-on and read-back to make sense of a passage I don't understand.			
• Know when I am unable to understand something and ask for help.			
• Visualise events and characters.			
I like: • Reading books by my favourite authors and trying others as well.			
• Recommending books I've enjoyed to my friends.			
• Telling why I did or didn't enjoy a book.			
• Being left in peace when I read.			
• Researching information.			
• Finding out about things and experiences which I'm not sure about.			
• Pretending I'm part of a story or one of the characters.			

Whole Class Profile Sheets

The class profile sheets have all indicators from the Reading Developmental Continuum presented phase-by-phase so that teachers can enter information about children's progress in reading. The sheets can be photocopied as required.

Why use Class Profile Sheets?

The class profile sheets enable teachers to develop a comprehensive class profile on which to base planning and programming decisions.

How to use the Class Profile Sheets?

- Observe children's reading behaviours
- Highlight indicators observed
- Write entry date and highlighter colour used

When would you use Class Profile Sheets?

Although teachers make ongoing observations of children's progress, they may formally update information on the continuum two or three times each year (perhaps before report times).

CLASS _____

ROLE PLAY READING INDICATORS

Student's Names

The Reader:

Making Meaning at Text Level

◆ displays – reading-like behaviour
   – holding the book the right way up
   – turning the pages appropriately
   – looking at words and pictures
   – using pictures to construct ideas

◆ realises that print carries a message but may read the writing differently each time, e.g. when 'reading' scribble to parents

◆ focuses on the meaning of a television program, story, or other text viewed, listened to or 'read'. Responses reflect understanding.

◆ makes links to own experience when listening to or 'reading' books, e.g. points to illustration, saying 'My dog jumps up too.'

• uses pictorial cues when sharing a book or 'reading', e.g. pointing to a picture in The Three Little Pigs, says 'The three little pigs left home.'

• turns the pages of a book, telling the story from memory

• knows that writing and drawing are different, e.g. 'Mummy reads the black bits.'

• selects favourite books from a range, e.g. chooses a book saying, 'I want The Three Little Pigs.'

• can talk about favourite stories and enjoys hearing them re-read

• is beginning to use some book language appropriately, e.g. 'Once upon a time...' The child may use a 'reading' voice

• responds to and uses simple terminology such as book, right way up, front, back, upside down

Making Meaning Using Context

◆ uses pictorial and visual cues when watching television, listening to or 'reading' stories, i.e. talks about a television program, advertisement or picture in a magazine or book, relating it to own knowledge and experience

• reacts to environmental print, e.g. noticing a fast food sign the child says 'I want a hamburger.'

Making Meaning at Word Level

◆ recognises own name, or part of it, in print

• is beginning to recognise some letters, e.g. Sam says 'That's my name', pointing to 'Stop' sign.

continued on next page
Teacher's Notes:
Dates:

CLASS _____

ROLE PLAY READING INDICATORS (continued)

Students' Names

The Reader:

Attitudes

- displays curiosity about print by experimenting with 'writing' and drawing and asking 'What does that say?'
- wants to look at books
- offers to 'read' writing and points to text while 'reading', indicating the beginning of having-a-go
- expresses enjoyment by joining in orally and responding emotively when listening to familiar stories
- eagerly anticipates book-reading events that are part of daily routine.

Teacher's Notes:

Dates:

CLASS

EXPERIMENTAL READING INDICATORS

Student's Names

The Reader:

Making Meaning at Text Level

◆ realises that print contains a constant message, i.e. that the words of a written story remain the same, but the words of an oral story may change

◆ is focused on expressing the meaning of a story rather than on reading words accurately

• knows that print goes from left to right and from top to bottom of a page

• responds to and uses terminology such as: letter, word, sentence, chapter

• is beginning to demonstrate awareness of literary language, e.g. 'a long, long time ago...', 'by the fire sat a cat', 'No, no, no', said the....'

• identifies the subject matter of a story through the use of titles and illustrations, e.g. 'I want the story about the big black cat'

• shows an ability to connect ideas and events from stories heard or viewed by retelling events in sequence, using pictures, memory of the story and knowledge of story structure

• expresses personal views about the actions of a character and speculates on own behaviour in a similar situation, e.g. 'If I had been...I would have...'

• sub-vocalises or whispers when reading 'silently'

Making Meaning Using Context

◆ uses prior knowledge of context and personal experience to make meaning, e.g. uses memory of a text to match spoken with written words

• demonstrates understanding of one-to-one correspondence between spoken and written words, for instance, the child slows down when dictating to an adult

• asks for assistance with some words. May be aware that own reading is not accurate and may seek help, re-read or stop reading

• uses patterns of language to predict words or phrases.

continued on next page

Teacher's Notes:

Date:

Whole Class Profile Sheet

CLASS _____

Students' Names

EXPERIMENTAL READING INDICATORS (continued)

The Reader:

Making Meaning at Word Level

◆ recognises some personally significant words in context, e.g. in a job roster, weather chart or books

◆ matches some spoken words with written words when reading a book or environmental print

• is developing the ability to separate a word from the object it represents. For instance, the child realises that 'Dad' is a little word, not that 'Dad' is a big word because Dad is big

• recognises some letters of the alphabet and is able to name them

• demonstrates some knowledge of letter-sound relationships, for instance, the sound represented by the initial and most salient letters in words

• points to specific known words as they are read

• uses initial letter sounds to predict words in texts

Attitudes

• is beginning to see self as a reader and talks about own reading

• may ask for favourite stories to be read and re-read

• joins in and acts out familiar stories if invited to do so

• selects books to read for pleasure

• self-selects texts on basis of interest or familiarity.

Teacher's Notes:

Dates:

CLASS

EARLY READING INDICATORS

Students' Names

The Reader:

Making Meaning at Text Level

◆ **is beginning to read familiar texts confidently and can retell major contents from visual and printed texts, e.g. language experience recounts, shared books, simple informational texts and children's television programs**

◆ **can identify and talk about a range of different text forms such as letters, lists, recipes, stories, newspaper and magazine articles, television dramas, and documentaries**

◆ **demonstrates understanding that all texts, both narrative and informational, are written by authors who are expressing their own ideas**

• identifies the main topic of a story or informational text and supplies some supporting information

• talks about characters in books using picture clues, personal experience and the text to make inferences

• provides detail about characters, setting and events when retelling a story

• talks about ideas and information from informational texts, making links to own knowledge

• has a strong personal reaction to advertisements, ideas and information from visual and written texts

• makes comparisons with other texts read or viewed. The reader's comments could relate to theme, setting, character, plot, structure, information or the way the text is written

• can talk about how to predict text content, e.g. 'I knew that book hadn't got facts in it. The dinosaurs had clothes on.'

continued on next page

Teacher's Notes:

Dates:

CLASS _____

EARLY READING INDICATORS (continued)

The Reader:

Making Meaning Using Context

◆ may read word-by-word or line-by-line when reading an unfamiliar text, i.e. reading performance may be word centred. Fluency and expression become stilted as the child focuses on decoding

◆ uses picture cues and knowledge of context to check understanding of meaning

• generally makes meaningful substitutions, however over-reliance on graphophonics may cause some meaning to be lost

• may sub-vocalise when reading difficult text 'silently'

• is beginning to use self-correction as a strategy

• uses knowledge of sentence structure and punctuation to help make meaning (syntactic strategies)

• sometimes reads-on to confirm meaning

• re-reads passage in order to clarify meaning that may have been lost due to word-by-word reading. May re-read a phrase, a sentence or a paragraph

• can talk about strategies used at the sentence level, e.g. 'If I think it doesn't sound right, I try again'

• is beginning to integrate prediction and substantiation

Making Meaning at Word Level

◆ has a bank of words which are recognised when encountered in different contexts, e.g. in a book, on the blackboard, in the environment or on a chart

◆ relies heavily on beginning letters and sounding-out for word identification (graphophonic strategies)

• carefully reads text, demonstrating the understanding that meaning is vested in the words

• may point as an aid to reading, using finger, eyes or voice, especially when reading difficult text

• locates words from sources such as word banks and environmental print

• when questioned can reflect on own word identification strategies, e.g. 'I sounded it out'.

continued on next page

Teacher's Notes:

Dates:

Students' Names

CLASS _____

EARLY READING INDICATORS (continued)

Students' Names																												
The Reader:																												
Attitude																												
• is willing to have-a-go at reading unknown words																												
• enjoys listening to stories																												
• reads for a range of purposes, e.g. for pleasure or information																												
• responds sensitively to stories read																												
• discusses favourite books																												
• talks about favourite author																												
• selects own reading material according to interest, purpose and level of difficulty and, with teacher support, can reconstruct information gained																												
Teacher's Notes:																												
Dates:																												

CLASS _____

TRANSITIONAL READING INDICATORS

Students' Names

The Reader:

Making Meaning at Text Level

◆ shows an ability to construct meaning by integrating knowledge of:

  – text structure, e.g. letter, narrative, report, recount, procedure

  – text organisation, e.g. paragraphs, chapters, introduction, conclusion, contents, page index

  – language features, e.g. descriptive language connectives such as because, therefore, if... then

  – subject specific language, e.g. the language of reporting in science and the language of a journalistic report

◆ can retell and discuss own interpretation of texts read or viewed with others, providing information relating to plot and characterisation in narrative or to main ideas and supporting detail in informational text

◆ recognises that characters can be stereotyped in a text, e.g. a mother looking after children at home while the father goes out to work or a prince rescuing a helpless maiden from an evil stepmother, and discusses how this could be changed

◆ selects appropriate material and adjusts reading strategies for different texts and purposes, e.g. skimming to search for a specific fact; scanning for a key word

• makes inferences and predictions based on information which is both explicit and implicit in a text

• makes generalisations based on interpretation of texts viewed or read, i.e. confirms, extends, or amends own knowledge through reading or viewing

• uses a range of strategies effectively to find relevant information in texts, e.g. makes use of table of contents and index

• reads orally with increasing fluency and expression. Oral reading reflects personal interpretation

• makes comparisons with other texts read

• selects texts effectively, integrating reading purpose and level of difficulty

• recognises devices which influence construction of meaning, such as the attribution of 'good' or 'bad' facial characteristics, clothing or language; and the provision of emotive music and colour; and stereotypical roles and situations in written or visual texts.

continued on next page

Teacher's Notes:

Date:

CLASS

Students' Names

TRANSITIONAL READING INDICATORS (continued)

The Reader:

Strategies for Making Meaning Using Context

◆ is becoming efficient in using most of the following strategies for constructing meaning:

– makes predictions and is able to substantiate them

– self-corrects when reading

– re-reads to clarify meaning

– reads-on when encountering a difficult text

– slows down when reading difficult texts

– substitutes familiar words

– uses knowledge of print conventions, e.g. capitalisation, full stops, commas, exclamation marks, speech marks

◆ makes meaningful substitutions, i.e. replacement miscues are meaningful, e.g. 'cool' drink for 'cold' drink. The integration of the three cuing systems (semantic, syntactic and graphophonic) is developing

• is able to talk about some of the strategies for making meaning

Making Meaning at Word Level

◆ has an increasing bank of sight words, including some difficult and subject-specific words, e.g. science, experiment, February, Christmas

◆ is becoming efficient in the use of the following word identification strategies for constructing meaning:

– sounds-out to decode words

– uses initial letters as a cue to decoding

– uses knowledge of common letter patterns to decode words, e.g. th, tion, scious, ough

– uses known parts of words to make sense of the whole word

– uses blending to decode words, e.g. str-ing

– uses word segmentation and syllabification to make sense of a whole word .

continued on next page

Teacher's Notes:

Dates:

CLASS _____

TRANSITIONAL READING INDICATORS (continued)

Student's Names

The Reader:

Attitude

- is self-motivated to read for pleasure
- reads for a range of purposes
- responds sensitively to stories
- discusses favourite books
- may discover a particular genre, e.g. adventure stories (may seek out other titles of this type)
- shows a marked preference for a specific type of book or author
- makes comparisons with other texts read
- demonstrates confidence when reading different texts.

Teacher's Notes:

Dates:

Whole Class Profile Sheet

© Education Department of Western Australia. Published by Addison Wesley Longman Australia 1994. This page may be photocopied for classroom use only.

CLASS

Students' Names

INDEPENDENT READING INDICATORS

The Reader:

Making Meaning at Text Level

- ◆ can recognise and discuss the elements and purposes of different text structures, e.g. reports, procedures, biographies, narratives, advertisements, dramas, documentaries

- ◆ reads and comprehends text that is abstract and removed from personal experience

- ◆ makes inferences based on implicit information drawn from a text and can provide justification for these inferences

- ◆ returns purposefully to make connections between widely separated sections of a text

- ◆ makes critical comparisons between texts

- ◆ can discuss an alternative reading of a text and offer possible reasons why a text may be interpreted differently by different readers or viewers

- • talks with others about interesting or difficult content

- • can justify own interpretation of a text

- • comments and makes judgements on the ways authors represent people from different cultural and socio-economic groups

- • is beginning to recognise and appreciate that authors manipulate language in a variety of ways to clarify and enhance meaning

- • can recognise and discuss the elements and purposes of different text structures, e.g. biography, mystery

- • reflects on and discusses issues and topics that have emerged when reading or viewing
  - – challenges and criticises text and topics, offering supportive evidence
  - – organises logical responses to a text
  - – selects relevant information for own purpose
  - – identifies and synthesises points of view
  - – draws conclusions from text and generalises about information extracted from them

- • may compare self and own experiences with fictional characters to enrich understanding

- • reads and comments critically on materials such as news items, magazine articles, advertisements and letters in the press, identifying techniques and features designed to influence readers

- • applies basic research skills effectively, e.g. identifies informational needs, uses knowledge of library organisation and text organisation and extracts relevant information from data base, catalogue or book.

continued on next page
Teacher's Notes:
Dates:

Whole Class Profile Sheet

CLASS _____

INDEPENDENT READING INDICATORS (continued)

Students' Names

The Reader:

Making Meaning Using Context

◆ uses a range of strategies automatically when constructing meaning from text

  – self-corrects

  – re-reads

  – reads-on

  – slows down

  – sub-vocalises

Making Meaning at Word Level

◆ uses word identification strategies appropriately and automatically when encountering an unknown word

  – knowledge of graphophonics

  – knowledge of word patterns

  – knowledge of word derivations, morphographs, prefixes, suffixes and syllabification

Attitude

• may avidly pursue a favourite author. Books may be compared and recommended to others

• feels strongly about reading preferences and can justify opinions

• is totally absorbed when reading

• sees books as a major source of information

• empathises strongly with admired characters in fiction.

Teacher's Notes:

Dates:

CLASS

ADVANCED READING INDICATORS

Students' Names

The Reader:

Making Meaning at Text Level

◆ critically reflects on and responds to text, providing different levels of interpretation and adopting alternative view-points

◆ can stand back and reflect on own reactions to authors' perceived ideologies and positions

◆ recognises specific language forms such as figurative language, jargon and technical language

◆ recognises and describes the purpose and structure of different genres

◆ reflects personal interpretation of a text through oral reading

◆ recognises and responds to text complexity, e.g. ambiguity and conflicting messages in text

◆ can compare and contrast different points of view

◆ can identify and integrate layers of facts and concepts within a text

◆ can identify and discuss different authors' styles

◆ can recognise texts as 'cultural constructs' and can analyse the cultural beliefs underpinning texts

◆ can synthesise information within and across texts

◆ is able to select, use, monitor and reflect on appropriate strategies for different reading purposes

◆ is able to interrogate texts, articulating problems and formulating relevant questions

◆ can select key information and ignore irrelevant material

◆ can apply understanding of text structure to the acquisition, organisation and application of information

◆ can formulate and apply research strategies

◆ can recognise and analyse bias, propaganda and stereotyping in texts

◆ can draw on literary and cultural repertoires to construct meanings in order to compare the perceived world view of an author with own.

continued on next page

Teacher's Notes:

Dates:

CLASS _____

ADVANCED READING INDICATORS (continued)

Students' Names

The Reader:

Attitude:

- uses reading to enter worlds beyond personal experience
- confidently handles new texts
- responds sensitively and perceptively to literature
- reads literature with emotional involvement and reflective detachment.

Teacher's Notes:

Dates:

Whole Class Profile Sheet

Whole Class Profile Sheets
Key Indicators Only

The whole class profile, key indicators only sheets show all key indicators from the six Reading Developmental Continuum phases.

Why use the Key Indicator Sheets?

The key indicators can be used by teachers to quickly ascertain children's stages of reading development and get an accurate class profile. The information can be used by teachers to plan future teaching and allocate resources appropriately.

How to use the Key Indicator Profile Sheet

- Observe children's reading behaviours
- Highlight indicators observed
- Write entry date and highlighter colour used

When would you use Indicator Profile Sheets?

Teachers may use these sheets to get a quick profile of a new class or to help when reporting to parents. Schools may decide on set times (say twice each year) for this information to be collected and analysed.

KEY INDICATORS

Phase 1: Role Play Reading

The Reader:

Making Meaning at Text Level

◆ displays reading-like behaviour
  – holding the book the right way up
  – turning the pages appropriately
  – looking at words and pictures
  – using pictures to construct ideas

◆ realises that print carries a message but may read the writing differently each time, e.g. when 'reading' scribble to parents

◆ focuses on the meaning of a television program, story, or other text viewed, listened to or 'read'. Responses reflect understanding.

◆ makes links to own experience when listening to or 'reading' books, e.g. points to illustration, saying 'My dog jumps up too.'

Making Meaning Using Context

◆ uses pictorial and visual cues when watching television, listening to or 'reading' stories, i.e. talks about a television program, advertisement or picture in a magazine or book; making inferences and relating it to own knowledge and experience

Making Meaning at Word Level

◆ recognises own name, or part of it, in print.

continued on next page

Teacher's Notes:

Dates:

Students' Names

Whole Class Profile Sheet Key Indicators Only

CLASS

KEY INDICATORS

Student's Names

Phase 2: Experimental Reading

The Reader:

Making Meaning at Text Level

◆ realises that print contains a constant message, i.e. that the words of a written story remain the same, but the words of an oral story may change

◆ is focused on expressing the meaning of a story rather than on reading words accurately

Making Meaning Using Context

◆ uses prior knowledge of context and personal experience to make meaning, e.g. uses memory of a text to match spoken with written words

Making Meaning at Word Level

◆ recognises some personally significant words in context, e.g. in a job roster, weather chart or books

◆ matches some spoken words with written words when reading a book or environmental print.

continued on next page

Teacher's Notes:

Dates:

KEY INDICATORS

Student's Names

Phase 3: Early Reading

The Reader:

Making Meaning at Text Level

◆ is beginning to read familiar texts confidently and can retell major content from visual and printed text, e.g. language experience recounts, shared books, simple informational texts and children's television programs

◆ demonstrates understanding that all texts, both narrative and informational, are written by authors who are expressing their own ideas

◆ can identify and talk about a range of different text forms such as letters, lists, recipes, stories, newspaper and magazine articles, television dramas and documentaries

Making Meaning Using Context

◆ may read word-by-word or line-by-line when reading an unfamiliar text, i.e. reading performance may be word centred. Fluency and expression become stilted as the child focuses on decoding

◆ uses picture cues, and knowledge of context to check understanding of meaning

Making Meaning at Word Level

◆ has a bank of words which are recognised when encountered in different contexts, e.g. in a book, on the blackboard, in the environment or on a chart

◆ relies heavily on beginning letters and sounding-out for word identification (graphophonic strategies).

continued on next page

Teacher's Notes:

Date:

Whole Class Profile Sheet Key Indicators Only

CLASS

KEY INDICATORS

Students' Names

Phase 4: Transitional Reading

The Reader:

Making Meaning at Text Level

◆ shows an ability to construct meaning by integrating knowledge of:

– text structure, e.g. letter, narrative, report, recount, procedure

– text organisation, e.g. paragraphs, chapters, introduction, conclusion, contents, page, index

– language features, e.g. descriptive language connectives such as because, therefore, if… then

– subject specific language, e.g. the language of reporting in science and the language of a journalistic report

◆ can retell and discuss own interpretation of texts read or viewed with others, providing information relating to plot and characterisation in narrative or to main ideas and supporting detail in informational text

◆ recognises that characters can be stereotyped in a text, e.g. a mother looking after children at home while the father goes out to work or a prince rescuing a helpless maiden from an evil stepmother, and discusses how this could be changed

◆ selects appropriate material and adjusts reading strategies for different texts and purposes, e.g. skimming to search for a specific fact; scanning for a key word

Strategies for Making Meaning Using Context

◆ is becoming efficient in using most of the following strategies for constructing meaning:

– makes predictions and is able to substantiate them

– self-corrects when reading

– re-reads to clarify meaning

– reads-on when encountering a difficult text

– slows down when reading difficult texts

– substitutes familiar words

– uses knowledge of print conventions, e.g. capitalisation, full stops, commas, exclamation marks, speech marks

◆ makes meaningful substitutions, i.e. replacement miscues are meaningful, e.g. 'cool' drink for 'cold' drink. The integration of the three cuing systems (semantic, syntactic and graphophonic) is developing.

continued on next page

Teacher's Notes:

Dates:

Students' Names

KEY INDICATORS

Phase 4: Transitional Reading (continued)

The Reader:

Making Meaning at Word Level

◆ has an increasing bank of sight words, including some difficult and subject-specific words, e.g. science, experiment, February, Christmas

◆ is becoming efficient in the use of the following word identification strategies for constructing meaning:
  – sounds-out to decode words
  – uses initial letters as a cue to decoding
  – uses knowledge of common letter patterns to decode words, e.g. th, tion, scious, ough
  – uses known parts of words to make sense of the whole word
  – uses blending to decode words, e.g. str-ing
  – uses word segmentation and syllabification to make sense of a whole word.

continued on next page

Teacher's Notes:

Date:

Whole Class Profile Sheet Key Indicators Only

KEY INDICATORS

Student's Names

Phase 5: Independent Reading

The Reader:

Making Meaning at Text Level

- can recognise and discuss the elements and purposes of different text structures, e.g. reports, procedures, biographies, narratives, advertisements, dramas, documentaries
- reads and comprehends text that is abstract and removed from personal experience
- makes inferences based on implicit information drawn from a text and can provide justification for these inferences
- returns purposefully to make connections between widely separated sections of a text
- makes critical comparisons between texts
- can discuss an alternative reading of a text and offer possible reasons why a text may be interpreted differently by different readers or viewers

Making Meaning Using Context

- uses a range of strategies automatically when constructing meaning from text
  - self-corrects
  - re-reads
  - reads-on
  - slows down
  - sub-vocalises

Making Meaning at Word Level

- uses word identification strategies appropriately and automatically when encountering an unknown word
  - knowledge of graphophonics
  - knowledge of word patterns
  - knowledge of word derivations, morphographs, prefixes, suffixes and syllabification.

continued on next page

Teacher's Notes:

Dates:

Whole Class Profile Sheet Key Indicators Only

Students' Names

Phase 6: Advanced																				
The Reader:																				
Making Meaning at Text Level																				
◆ critically reflects on and responds to text, providing different levels of interpretation and adopting alternative view-points																				
◆ can stand back and reflect on own reactions to authors' perceived ideologies and positions																				
◆ recognises specific language forms such as figurative language, jargon and technical language																				
◆ recognises and describes the purpose and structure of different genres																				
◆ reflects personal interpretation of a text through oral reading																				
◆ recognises and responds to text complexity, e.g. ambiguity and conflicting messages in text																				
◆ can compare and contrast different points of view																				
◆ can identify and integrate layers of facts and concepts within a text																				
◆ can identify and discuss different authors' styles																				
◆ can recognise texts as 'cultural constructs' and can analyse the cultural beliefs underpinning texts																				
◆ can synthesise information within and across texts																				
◆ is able to select, use, monitor and reflect on appropriate strategies for different reading purposes																				
◆ is able to interrogate texts, articulating problems and formulating relevant questions																				
◆ can select key information and ignore irrelevant material																				
◆ can apply understanding of text structure to the acquisition, organisation and application of information																				
◆ can formulate and apply research strategies																				
◆ can recognise and analyse bias, propaganda and stereotyping in texts																				
◆ can draw on literary and cultural repertoires to construct meanings in order to compare the perceived world view of an author with own.																				
Teacher's Notes:																				
Dates:																				

Acknowledgements

The First Steps Developmental Continua were written by the FIRST STEPS TEAM under the direction of Alison Dewsbury.

The Reading Developmental Continuum was researched and written by Diana Rees, Education Officer, First Steps Project, Ministry of Education in collaboration with Dr Bruce Shortland-Jones, Senior Lecturer, School of Curriculum Studies, Curtin University of Technology.

We gratefully acknowledge the work of :
Jack Thomson (NSW) for his contribution to the Independent and Advanced phases of the Reading Continuum.
Beverly Broughton (QLD) for her ideas on reading development.
Caroline Barratt-Pugh for her contribution on working with children for whom English is a second language.
Kerry Misich and Rebecca Wright for their early work in the development of this book.
Kay Kovalevs for her dedication and hard work in the editing and coordination of the First Steps books in the early years of the project.

The First Steps project acknowledges the invaluable contributions made by the schools and teachers listed below and by all the school principals who have supported their staffs as they participated in the First Steps Project:
- Challis Early Childhood Education Centre
- Grovelands Early Childhood Education Centre
- Tuart Hill Junior Primary School
- Glen Forrest Primary School
were involved in action research that focused on the use of different Continua.

The Project received a great deal of assistance from the following Primary Schools:
- Carey Park Primary School
- Hollywood Primary School
- Medina Primary School
- Midvale Primary School
- Mingenew Primary School
- West Busselton Primary School
- Wilson Primary School
- Kalgoorlie Central Primary School
- Boulder Primary School
- Boulder Junior Primary School.

The Project is also grateful to **Wagin District High School** in the Narrogin District and the schools in the Esperance District—the **Bremer Bay, Castletown, Condingup, Esperance, Fitzgerald, Gairdner, Grass Patch, Jerdacuttup, Lake King, Munglinup, Nulsen, Ongerup and Varley Primary Schools**, which, with **Jerramungup** and **Ravensthorpe District High Schools**, achieved so much in an associate role between 1989 and 1991. These schools provided examples of exemplary practice and documentation that enabled the Project team to refine and extend aspects of First Steps.

The Gosnells Oral Language Project was initiated by **Wirrabirra Education Support Unit** and Ashburton Drive, **Gosnells, Huntingdale, Seaforth** and **Wirrabirra Primary Schools** under the leadership of **Leanne Allen** and **Judith Smailes**. First Steps supported this project with funding, editorial and publishing assistance.

First Steps and Aboriginal Children

Warakurna, Wingellina and **Blackstone Schools** took part in the **Ngaanyatjarra Lands Project** coordinated by Sandi Percival. Action research was carried out in these schools, evaluating the use of the First Steps Developmental Continua and related materials with children from the Central Desert.
Fitzroy Crossing District High School, Gogo and **Wangkajungka Primary Schools** participated in a special project designed to adapt the Continua and strategies to the needs of children in Kimberley schools. **Margi Webb** and **Chris Street** worked with colleagues to accomplish this task.
The following schools also addressed the literacy learning of Aboriginal students as part of a special project: in the **Narrogin District, Narrogin Primary School** and **Pingelly** and **Wagin District High Schools**; in the

Kalgoorlie District, **Menzies Primary School** and **Laverton** and **Leonora District High Schools** in the Karratha District, **Roebourne** and **Onslow Primary Schools**; in the Kimberley District, **Dawul** and **Jungdranung Primary Schools** and **Kununurra District High School**; and in the Bayswater District, **Midvale Primary School**.

First Steps and Children for whom English is a Second Language

The Highgate Primary School, with its **Intensive Language Centre**, has undertaken a special project designed to ensure that First Steps meets the needs of children for whom English is a second or foreign language. **Anna Sinclair** was the coordinator of this Project. **Kay Kovalevs** also contributed to and collated the ESL research into children's language learning at **Christmas Island District High School**.

Finally, special thanks must go to the children who have contributed their ideas.

Bibliography

Cambourne, B. 1988, *The Whole Story - Natural Learning and the Acquisition of Literacy in the Classroom,* Ashton Scholastic, Sydney.

Chall, J. 1984, *Stages of Reading Development,* McGraw Hill, New York, USA.

Curtin University of Technology 1988, *Language In-service Course (LINC),* Ministry of Education, Perth.

Education Department of South Australia 1978, *Resource Book on the Development of Reading Skills,* Carroll's Educational Publications, Adelaide.

Education Department of Tasmania 1988, *Pathways of Language Development,* Education Department of Tasmania, Hobart.

Education Department of Western Australia 1987, *Reading to Learn in the Secondary School,* Education Department of Western Australia, Perth.

Education Department of Western Australia 1988, *Management and Resources in the Early Years,* Education Department of Western Australia, Perth.

Education Department of Western Australia 1993, *Reading K-7 Teachers Notes,* Education Department of Western Australia, Perth.

Glazer, S., Searfoss, L. and Gentile, L. (eds) 1988, *Re-examining Reading Diagnosis New Trends and Procedures,* International Reading Association, Delaware, USA.

Holdaway, D. 1972, *Independence in Reading. A handbook on individualised procedures,* Ashton Scholastic, Auckland, NZ.

Kemp, M. 1987, *Watching Children Read and Write Observational Records for Children with Special Needs,* Nelson, Melbourne.

Mason, J. and Au, K. 1986, *Reading Instruction for Today,* Scott, Foresman & Co., Glenview, Illinois, USA.

McCracken, M.J. and R.A. 1979, *Reading Writing & Language A Practical Guide for Primary Teachers,* Peguis Publishers, Winnipeg, Canada.

Sloan, P. and Latham, R. 1981, *Teaching Reading IS,* Thomas Nelson, Melbourne.

Thomson, J. 1987, *Understanding Teenagers' Reading and Writing Processes and the Teaching of Literature,* Methuen, North Ryde, NSW.

Weaver, C. 1988, *Reading Process and Practice: from socio-psycholinguistics to whole language,* Heinemann Books, Portsmouth, New Hampshire, USA.